bloom

book

4 introduction
blooming inspiration

6 a return to roots
and other earthly matters

26 the need for green
and its peaceful benefits

46 the beauty of nature
and botanical well-being

68 an eye for composition
and the creative consumer

92 a look at volume
and the sculptural potential of plants

118 a quest for freshness
and the spring of spontaneity

144 the heart of the matter
and a garden of textures

170 the new art nouveau
and natural versus virtual

192 credits & captions

book
horti-culture for
the 21st century
by Li Edelkoort

With introductions to each chapter
by Li Edelkoort, text by Lisa White and
creative direction by Nelson Sepulveda

Flammarion

BLOOMING INSPIRATION Like Bloom magazine, this first Bloom Book gives a new and unique sense to the contemplation of nature, a way to embrace plants and flowers with a fresh eye and to witness how much the natural world inspires, and even takes inspiration from, the rest of the creative world.

As a trend forecaster, I have noticed over the years how trends come and go and influence our relationships with flowers and plants. Increasingly, flowers, plants and trees–all natural matter in fact–form an intrinsic part of our changing lifestyles, intimately linked with all other interests in life, like art, design, food, free time, friends, family and philosophy.

Indeed, the horticulture industry is becoming a full-blown lifestyle industry in its own right, taking and giving inspiration to all other industries, which share this information in turn: flowers inspire fabrics, fabrics inspire shapes, shapes inspire vases, vases inspire volumes, volumes inspire flowers, flowers inspire food, food inspires fashion, fashion inspires industrial design, design inspires florists, florists inspire consumers, consumers inspire each other and, ultimately, the horticulture industry.

At this intersection of industries, disciplines and players, the Bloom Book fits in as an inspirational tool. Not only do we want to forecast colours, bouquets, bulbs, recipients, hybrids and gardens but we wish to uncover the horti-culture within a larger, universal culture.

This is why we cover floral artists and artists working with flowers; this is why we discuss the symbolism of species, healing with nature, edible blossoms, and new hybrids, surpassing reality with imaginative and personal points of view.

Over the last years the interest in flowers and gardening has grown to unbelievable proportions. Gardening is the fastest-developing hobby on our planet; it is a global trend. Even in Japan it is the movement of the moment though few people have gardens and no one has extra space.

We believe the world's interest in flowers, plants and gardening is here to stay, heralding a new millennium where we will further integrate nature into our lives, creating even closer ties with living matter, embracing beauty every day.

Li Edelkoort

a return to **roots**

and other earthly matters

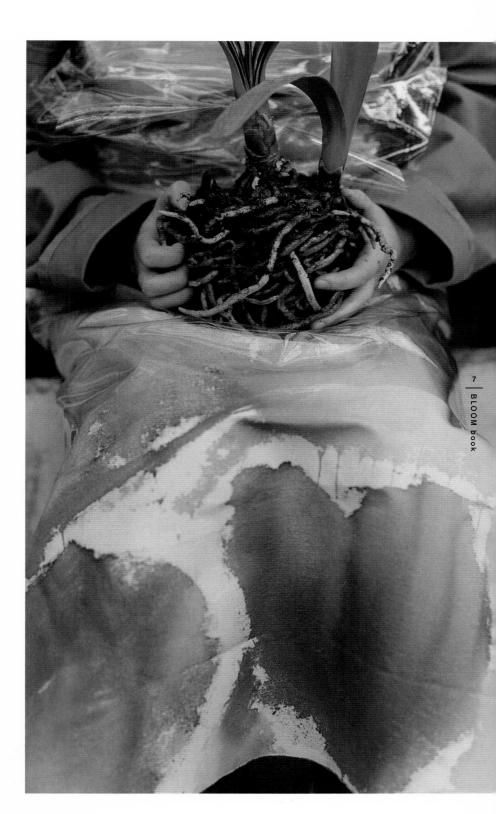

We needed inspiration from horses and birds to design cars and aeroplanes, from forests and mountains to create city canyons, and from bees and ants to develop industry; a clever concept organised to supply labour to produce goods and to generate income for hardworking classes to consume. Indeed, from the Industrial Age onwards, we felt like gods, able to re-create everything on earth.

Then, we grew tired of working hard so we invented the weekend and summer holidays, in order to return to our senses and get back to nature through camping, picnicking, pony rides and beach strolls. To experience nature, if in a semi-artificial and encapsulated manner.

More years passed of ups and downs, of society getting richer and life getting poorer. Man made so much that nature started to speak up and warn us, with disappearing species, torrential rains and melting ice caps. We began to realise that too much greed and too many choices were going to jeopardise the earth and its inhabitants. Therefore, man invented a system of communication, where we would trade ideas and knowledge through an immaterial web called the Internet. The virtual world was born and we began to truly experience the global village. Again, we felt a little more like gods.

However, living in a virtual society has proved to be difficult and alien to us. Using this advanced system of communication, we have lost our sense of smell and touch and taste. Today, we seek to change our lifestyles, searching for emotion, rediscovering the sensations of the early earth. We are in the process of going back to our roots, of getting in touch with our primitive pasts and acknowledging our primal behaviour patterns. We want to return our feet to the ground, to take root again.

This is why roots are becoming a focus in horticulture, symbolising this return to the earth, this quest for a forgotten paradise and meaning. Furthermore, roots are increasingly becoming part of our lifestyles. Roots, bulbs and tubers are welcomed on our plates. Roots are inspiration for unbridled organic studies in shape. Roots are a source of design and beauty but also play an important part in alternative healing, composing concoctions that strengthen our nerves or act as powerful aphrodisiacs. Roots will also invade the cosmetic industry and will empower new fragrances.

Roots will increasingly become an integral part of our lives, wiring us to the earth while connecting the past with the future.

- L.E.

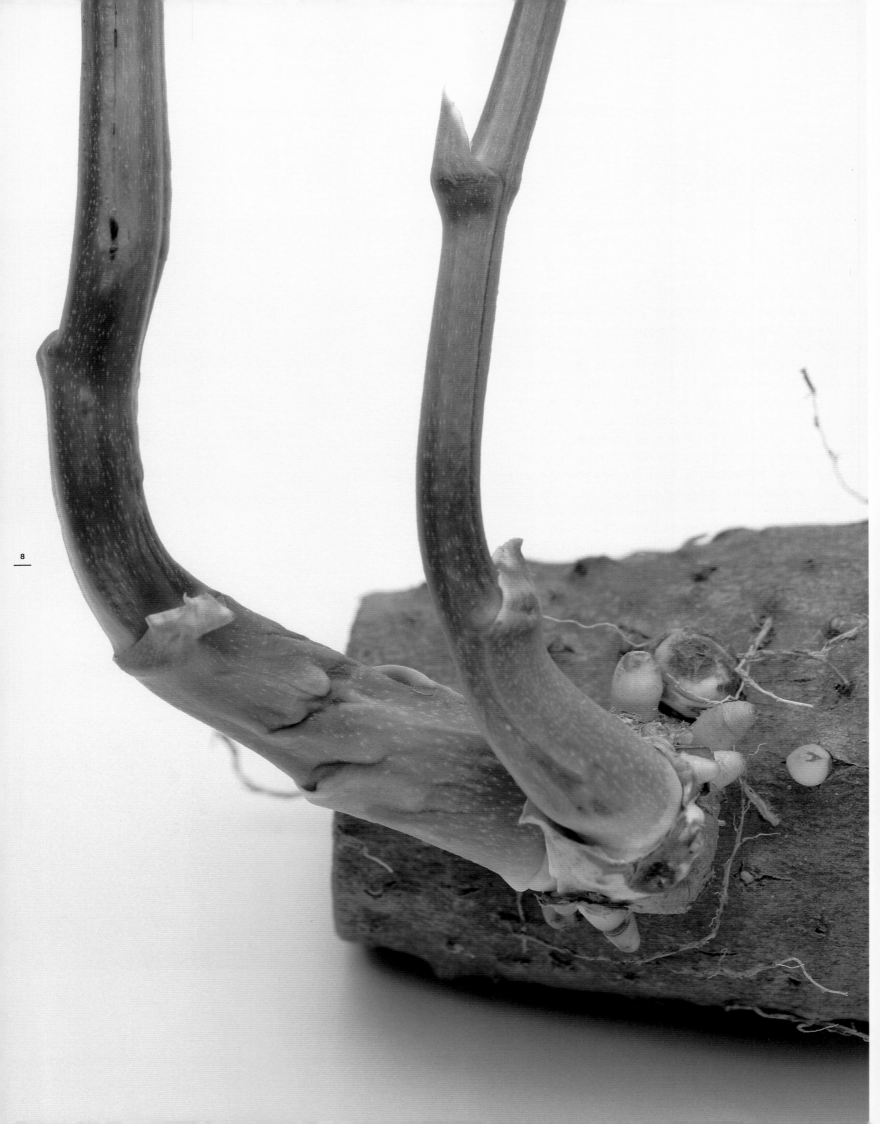

he Gaia principle advocates a planet earth which embraces all realms and origins, both plant and animal, creating a sense of harmony which is perfectly contained in the very definition of a root as *the essential part or nature of something.*

As technology, finance and communications transform the world into a global village, we become increasingly conscious of a notion of our shared planet, of a need for wholeness, reminiscent of generous Gaia, earth goddess from Greek mythology. We could consider the animal and plant realms as being a kind of 'interface' within her body. As such, "Where humanity and plants meet, a synergistic energy can be created and exchanged. . . . We then have an ecologically integrated process that heals and harmonises the inner environment (the human body) whilst being produced by an outer harmonised environment (nature)."[1]

In a similar manner, roots are our interface with the earth. And when we speak of roots, we must first think of the soil itself, the rich loam or rough clay that supports us physically and nutritionally. Soil is a fusion of mineral and organic matter, housing up to a billion micro-organisms per gram. According to agronomic engineer Dr Claude Bourguignon, 'Despite its appearing a rather inhospitable place to foster life, the ground accommodates the greater part of the living biomass of the planet. This swarming of organisms that we trample on every day is a bit like the primordial soup from which life first emerged; it is the bases of all biological processes. . . .

This discreet, invisible world plays a fundamental role in the development of life on earth.'[2] Roots are indispensable in creating a quality soil, for they take food from the earth yet also enrich it, breaking up and airing the dirt by infiltrating it with their members, which also secrete carbon-rich exudates that allow beneficial microbes to develop. Upon the death of the plant, the roots decompose to create rich humus, further benefiting the soil. Some roots, like the anthropomorphic mangrove, which grows in the world's marshes and tidal shores, actually help create soil. Referred to as 'island makers', they grow in shallow waters, catching dirt in their interlacing, above-ground roots, permitting land to amass—sometimes rapidly enough to be visible to the naked eye. Alexander the Great is said to have halted his march through Asia in order to watch mangroves making land.

The root itself is a fascinating organism—either sinuous, elongated or round, yet always voluptuous—and thanks to which a plant is not only anchored in the ground but fed as well by its natural absorption of water and mineral salts. Roots differ in kind: there are adventitious roots which grow on the side of the stem (as on ivy) or on rhizomes which are often horizontal (like the iris); aerial roots, equal fascicled roots to which category leeks belong; fleshy tubers like carrots and potatoes and the tap-root which is a main, vertical root. It is nearly impossible to dig up an entire root, so delicate is its network-like structure, so that one is surprised to learn the length, and indeed depth, of even the most common roots.

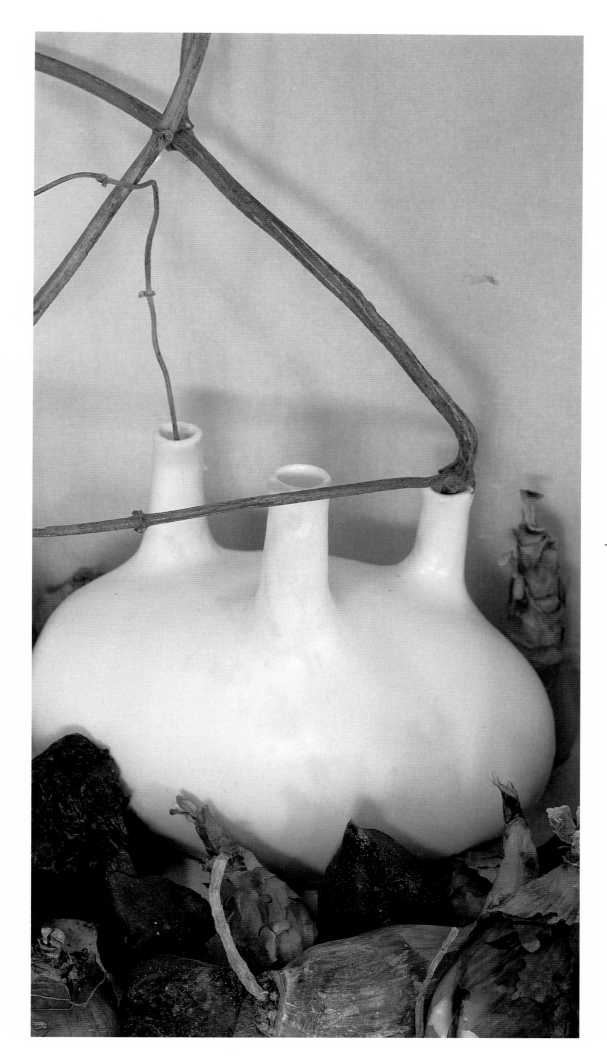

A stalk of wheat can have deeper roots that that of an oak tree, and lucerne can grow roots up to ten metres long. Plants stock nourishment in their roots which grow deep in the earth, protected from light, providing a life-support system. A system which requires a full vegetation cycle to become edible, as vegetable root seeds are sown in springtime and dug up for food in late autumn and winter. Roots have been part of our nutrition since the beginning of mankind. Food roots were domesticated in New Guinea in the late Palaeolithic age, about 10 000 years B.C., and in the Near East traces of wild parsnip consumption have been found from the late Mesolithic age on, about 2 000 years BC. The importance of root gathering is not to be dismissed: searching the soil was the first gesture which would ultimately lead mankind to agriculture.

One tuber in particular still constitutes a staple of our diet: the common, or garden, potato. Brought by Spaniards back to Europe from South America in the second half of the 16th century, the potato had to wait until 1789 and the French Revolution to be officially introduced in France by Parmentier in his *Traité sur la culture et son usage*. But not without a certain upheaval. The tuber's odyssey is both well-known and revealing: Parmentier, imprisoned in Westphalia during the Seven Year's War, where his primary concern was to be able to eat to survive, had been fed potatoes by his German captors. These latter (like the French) considered the lowly tuber to be a harbinger of disease, edible only for animals—and prisoners.

Much to his surprise, Parmentier was not only pleased to eat them, he also survived to sing their praise. People were starving at that time and it was to remedy the famine—hoping to overcome the potato's bad reputation—that Parmentier wrote the treaty upon his return in 1763. The problem was that most of the starving, the French peasants, were illiterate and only knew about the tuber's disfavour, an example of which was the Besançon parliament's banning of its cultivation. Coaxing a famished peasant population to consume the disdained spud was no mean feat. Presented as 'economical rice', it was given by the priest of Saint-Roch in Paris in 1769 to his parishioners. Although acclaimed by Mirabeau 'comparable to the best soups', it still didn't tempt the peasants. Parmentier, who never gave up hope, called on Louis XVI for help and the willing King planted a potato patch in Neuilly. When the tubers were ripe, he had his guard surround the potato patch, mounting fake surveillance. Nothing more was required to entice the peasants to appropriate the contents of the royal vegetable garden and the humble tuber found its way to hungry bellies.

The undeniably nutritive properties of roots can be equalled only by another of their surprising attributes: their medicinal and healing possibilities. The Chinese have an ancient tradition of prevention and healing with plants and their roots.

However, in the Occident, we are still too estranged from our own roots to fully take advantage of their curative properties. There are of course folk remedies and decoctions but many people tend to be wary of old lore—even when based upon good sense—and any medication which is not purchased at the drug store. Yet herbal medicine can be potent, either preventing disease or helping to strengthen and balance the body when confronted with serious illness. Numerous roots contribute their beneficial properties to herbal remedies: the Blood root *(Sanguinaria canadensis)* treats bronchitis, asthma, croup and laryngitis; Blue flag *(Iris versicolor)* is a skin remedy for everything from blemishes to eczema since it helps detoxify the liver, Carline thistle *(Carlina vulgaris)* has considerable antiseptic properties and as such is used for healing wounds; Ginger *(Zingiber officinale)* treats bad circulation, cramps and colic, and Ginseng *(Panax ginseng)* can be used as a remedy against states of exhaustion, weakness or depression and can raise lowered blood pressure to normal levels.

Good old Garlic (*Allium sativum*)
has polyvalent properties which are
universally recognised: it is one of
the most effective anti-microbial
plants treating chronic bronchitis,
recurrent colds and flu. It has also
been known to reduce blood pressure
and cholesterol levels over a period
of time—in short, a perfect first
aid kit.

Indeed, roots are a source of
human energy and aid, and should
be the centre of attention. This
wealth is poised, after years of
neglect, to see the light—and why not
the spotlight? For years, society has
extolled the beauty of the flower's
corolla but now the indications
are united for a shift in style. Our
passion for gardening makes us
long for the lines of roots, for the
strength of fibrous strands which
bind us closer to the earth, for the
sensual pleasure of contemplating
the generous, round shape of the
Ypomoea root which looks like a
fertility symbol.

In textiles, this new approach
translates into woven fibres that
resemble roots, keeping us in touch
with rough, organic textures. In
cuisine, root vegetables, from
Jerusalem artichokes to parsnips,
tempt us, their myriad tastes combining with their rich vitamins
and minerals to help us flourish.
In fashion, we return to our sources,
blending ethnic and folkloric
design with our own cultural roots
to create a contemporary fusion
of near and far, past and present.

In decoration, roots are becoming increasingly prevalent. Discarding traditional bouquets, we are more inclined to place a willowy root in a vase or make a still-life with an assortment of roots and gourds, their squash and marrow cousins from the vegetable garden, creating an infinite variety of size, colour, shape and texture in both natural and nature-inspired materials.

In such a way, a root is a quintessential and timeless marvel of nature, a thing of innate magnificence. The plant world has preceded us on this earth for millions of years, providing us the oxygen we breathe, much of the food we eat, the shelter we seek and the medicine we need. A fact which, like roots themselves, we have often taken for granted. However, once grounded by the presence of our roots—worldly, cultural and spiritual—we can achieve a new feeling of balance and belonging, with our feet firmly planted in the earth to attain a harmony which, in the long run, will be beneficial to a planet in need of increasing attention from mankind in order to survive. ■

Notes

[1] **Hoffmann**, David
The Holistic Herbal
The Findhorn Press

[2] **Bourguignon**, Claude
Le sol, la terre et les champs;
de l'agronomie à l'agrologie
Sang de la Terre, Paris, 1996

Other sources

Danneyrolles, Jean-Luc
Un Jardin Extraordinaire
Actes Sud, Arles, 2001

Goust, Jérome
La Carotte et le Panais
Actes Sud, Arles, 2001

de Scitivaux, Armelle
L'Almanach du Gastronome
Les Editions du Bottin Gourmand
Paris, 1998

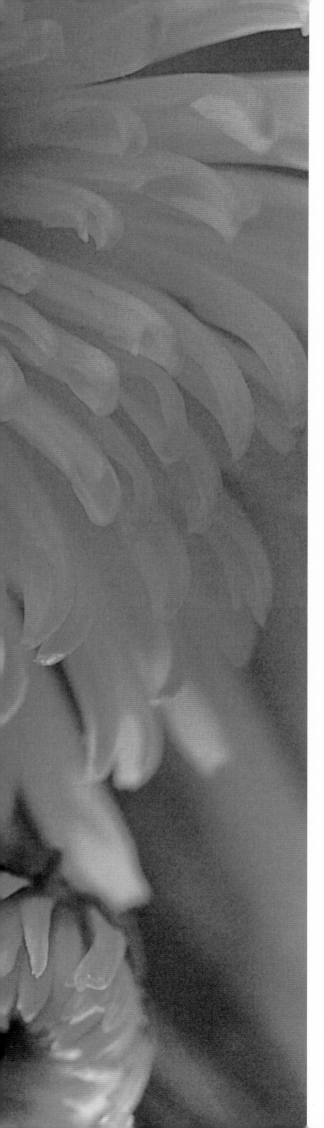

the need for
green

and its peaceful benefits

In the beginning green was designed to become the canvas of all colours: green pastures, forests, leaves and mosses served as a backdrop for flowers and fruits, birds and butterflies, animals and humans. Oranges, yellows, reds and pinks felt embellished and empowered in its decor, using green as a screen to become even more vainly beautiful themselves.

But, one day, green became self-conscious and decided the time had come to speak up and become a colour in its own right, with its own life and role to play. Only green knows how to give a new existence to a product, whether produced by man or by nature, and green is learning how to adapt to new surfaces, surprising categories and unusual spaces. Green is healthy for plastic, young on velvet, fresh in packaging, new in clothes and surprising in flowers. Green refreshes an old-fashioned chrysanthemum, ennobles the always-red amaryllis and renders the rose organic and natural.

Contemporary tales of science fiction naturally use synthetic greens to describe aliens visiting planet Earth, which makes green a fictional as well as a natural colour. Green is a mediating colour, hovering between hot and cold, high and low, old and new. Green is a provocative and complex colour, always bridging total extremes, as in the naive green of budding life and the deep, dusty green of decay. Green creates a balance, forms an interface between humans and nature (and perhaps other natures). Green is the grass invading our houses, industrial design, even growing on art; green is an apple, symbol of health and wholesomeness, decorating our fabrics and animating our kitchen tables; green is moss, discreetly and mysteriously covering our gardens and colouring our couches; green is leaves, feeding our brains and packaging our foods. Our desire for green is tinting our fingers and colouring our environments. In green we trust.

A colour that becomes the brand of a political movement must have powerful things to convey. A vision of the future with man and nature living in awe of each other, being in love with each other—a wish for paradise regained.

- L.E.

reen is often cited as one of the least-appreciated colours, yet it is the shade we cannot live without. Green is a colour we need, bringing us physical—and mental—oxygen. The noted gardener and writer Donald Culross Peattie once said 'Plant life sustains the living world—more precisely, chlorophyll does so. Blood, bone and sinew, all flesh is grass.'

Complementing the red blood in our veins, the green of chlorophyll is vital to our sustenance. Indeed, the composition and function of chlorophyll and human blood closely resemble one another, though chlorophyll colours leaves green and hemin colours blood red, though chlorophyll contains magnesium where hemin contains iron. The close physical relationship between chlorophyll and blood, between flora and fauna, is based on the process called photosynthesis, the life-support system of a plant, a flower, a tree, and ultimately, the entire earth. Leaves convert the sun's energy into food for the plant, creating oxygen in the process—a by-product indispensable to the blood and thus to the survival of animals and people.

Chlorophyll combines the energy of light from the sun with carbon dioxide from the air (given off as a by-product from human and animal energy creation) and with the minerals and water sent up by the plants' roots. The reaction of all these processes and substances produces starch and sugar for the growth of the plant, which enables it to produce even more chlorophyll-generating green leaves.

The verdant richness of plant life benefits us directly through our consumption of leaves, vegetables and fruits. According to naturopath Stevo Solaja, 'Colour is a biological food and is thus indispensable to our organism. Flowers, fruits and vegetables are coloured for a very good reason. Sunlight can be broken down into different colours, each of which has a certain frequence, a certain wavelength and energy. Through photosynthesis, plants transform light into food and in turn become food for us.'[1]

Dietetic and biological engineers Jacques and Patrice Mariot claimed that 'a food, to be considered thus, must be "alive"'[2]. And what is more alive than just-picked greens, be they peppery rocket lettuce, plump peas or asparagus? Vivid green wheatgrass juice is extolled by the health-conscious as the elixir of energy and youth. Young sprouts are rich in vitamins and minerals, bringing the force of green to our diets in winter when little fresh green is available. In fact, Solaja uses a diet of such greens to successfully treat patients with nervous and stress disorders, a so-called 'green cure'. Green heals, and it is thus the symbolic colour of pharmacies the world over.

Studies have shown that colours have similar benefits in clothing and in our environments as in food. Warm colours stimulate activity while cool colours calm and relax us. Green is a particularly important shade because it sits between the cool and the warm colours on the scale and thus plays a stabilising role. According to Solaja, 'Sitting in a green room, wearing a green shirt, meditating upon the greenery of the garden or eating green beans puts us back into balance with ourselves and nature, and does a lot of good to the nervous system.' Edwin D. Babbitt, a scientist and mystic of the Victorian era, found that green lowers blood pressure, is sedative and hypnotic, helping both headaches and exhaustion. Proven by researchers to be the colour most beneficial to the intellect, Faber Birren, one of the fathers of colour psychology, concluded that 'Green provides an ideal environment for sedentary tasks, concentration and meditation.'[2] Correspondingly, Birren was able to reduce fatigue and improve concentration in the workers of an American textile mill by painting the end walls green.

A more widespread example is the serene shade of 'hospital green' that is now a standard in the health care profession.

Using shades of green in our homes—whether in the form of plants or in materials such as plastics, glass, paint or textiles—our tables become gardens of delight, our bathrooms become ponds of reflection, our living rooms become parks of pleasure and our bedrooms transform into oases of calm. We pop seaweed tablets into our tubs, place green plants next to our green computers, and take green herbs from our kitchens into our bedrooms to inhale the soothing scents of mint and thyme from the coolness of green sheets. The artist and writer Barbara Nemitz states in *Transplant,* her book on living vegetation in contemporary art, that 'The house is a garden. . . . Indeed, aren't the expansive patches of decorative fabrics actually flower beds? And wallpaper and embroideries are landscapes. . . . And the networks of cables and pipes—do they not spread throughout the house like parts of an organism? Are they not a root system in their own right?'[3] Taking this image further, young designers now incorporate growing grass into tables to permit 'al fresco' dining inside, and into carpets to tickle the senses. Moving the outside inside, our lifestyles are witnessing a green revolution. Hothouses, terrariums, potted plants, hanging gardens—people will do anything to get plants growing inside as well as outside, in order to live with the vibrant rhythms of their growing season.

And how does our garden—whether inside or out—grow? How does one obtain the much-coveted green thumb that insures luxuriant vegetation? Indeed, having a 'green thumb', 'green fingers' or a 'green hand' is an expression found in languages all across the globe.

Those gardeners with green thumbs insist that it is part intuition, part attention, and part hard work. Jean-Marie Pelt, the author of *The Secret Languages of Nature* maintains that 'A green thumb is nothing other than the combination between theoretical fact and empirical knowledge resulting from experience, all of this combined with a keen sense of observation, tenderness and a great deal of love.'[4]

And what sort of flowers do the green thumbs of this world want to grow? Green ones, of course. Green flowers have been around for millennia, but their popularity is rapidly increasing: we can now enjoy the 'Green Jeans' gladiola, green anthuriums or 'Shamrock' chrysanthemums. With their vivid green petals, these flowers seem forever young. To meet consumer demand, hybridists have been working hard to produce new green varieties. After 20 years of development, the 'Emerald' rose, launched in 1997, is one of the most notable of these hybrids, with tender green, beautifully formed petals, and has recently been followed by the green 'Kilimanjaro' rose. Another flower that we most often see in red, the amaryllis, now has its lush, green counterpart as well. The 'Green Amaryllis', with its creamy verdant petals, is now becoming a favourite holiday flower, taking the four weeks of Advent to achieve a full green bloom on Christmas Day. Like the Christmas tree, the green of this amaryllis brings us a message of hope and life in the dead of winter. Indeed, the appeal of the proverbial white Christmas has taken a backseat to a green, botanical Christmas, with not only evergreens but green flowers, green decorations in organic shapes, and even aquatic plants.

Beyond flowers, leaves are also elements to be contemplated and elevated to a higher status. Not just the workers of the natural world, leaves have aesthetic forms and textures that can outshine the beauty of many a flower. 'Leaves are of more various forms than the alphabets of all languages put together,' claimed Henry David Thoreau.

40

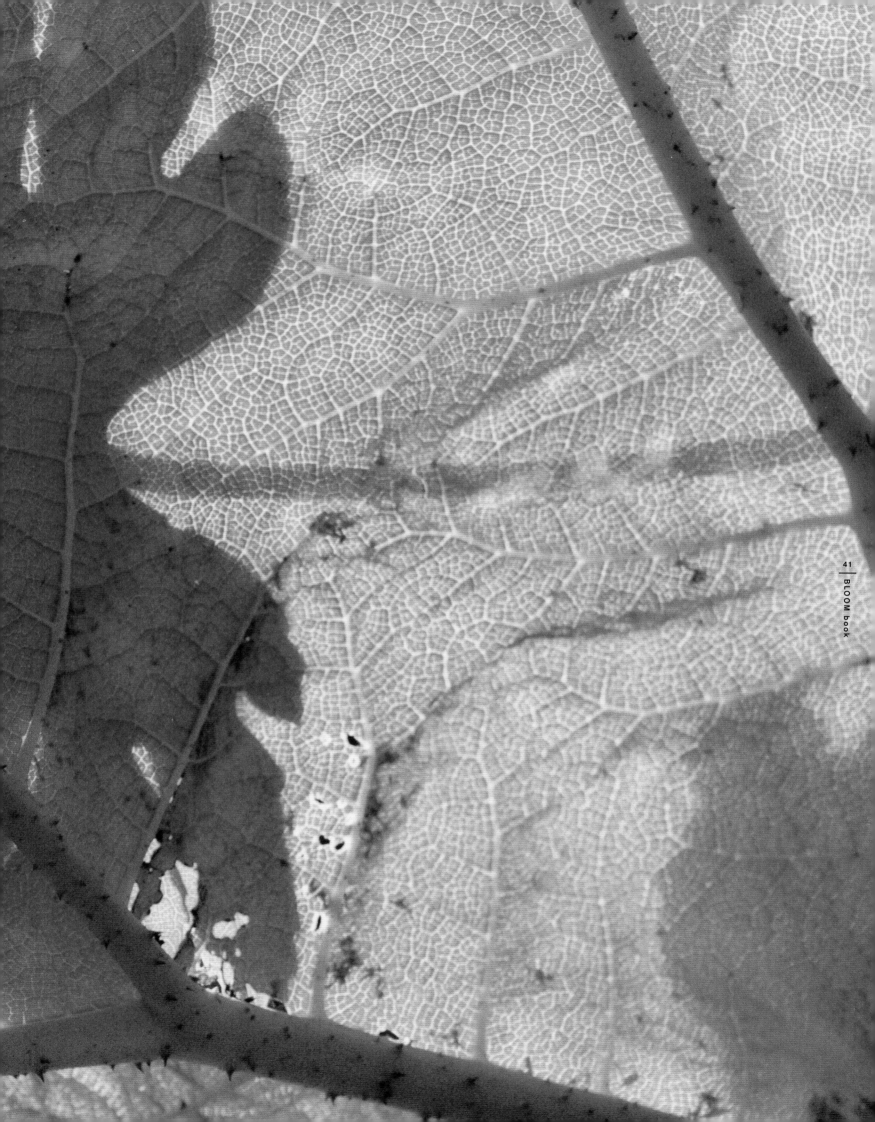

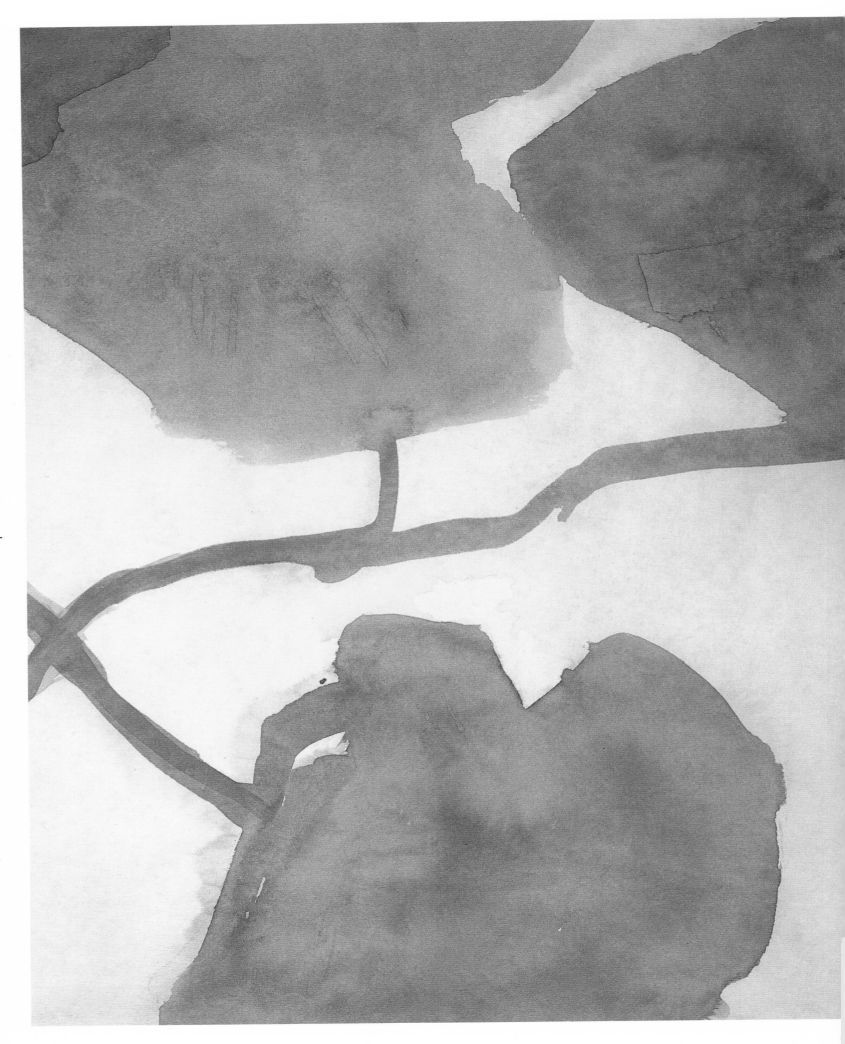

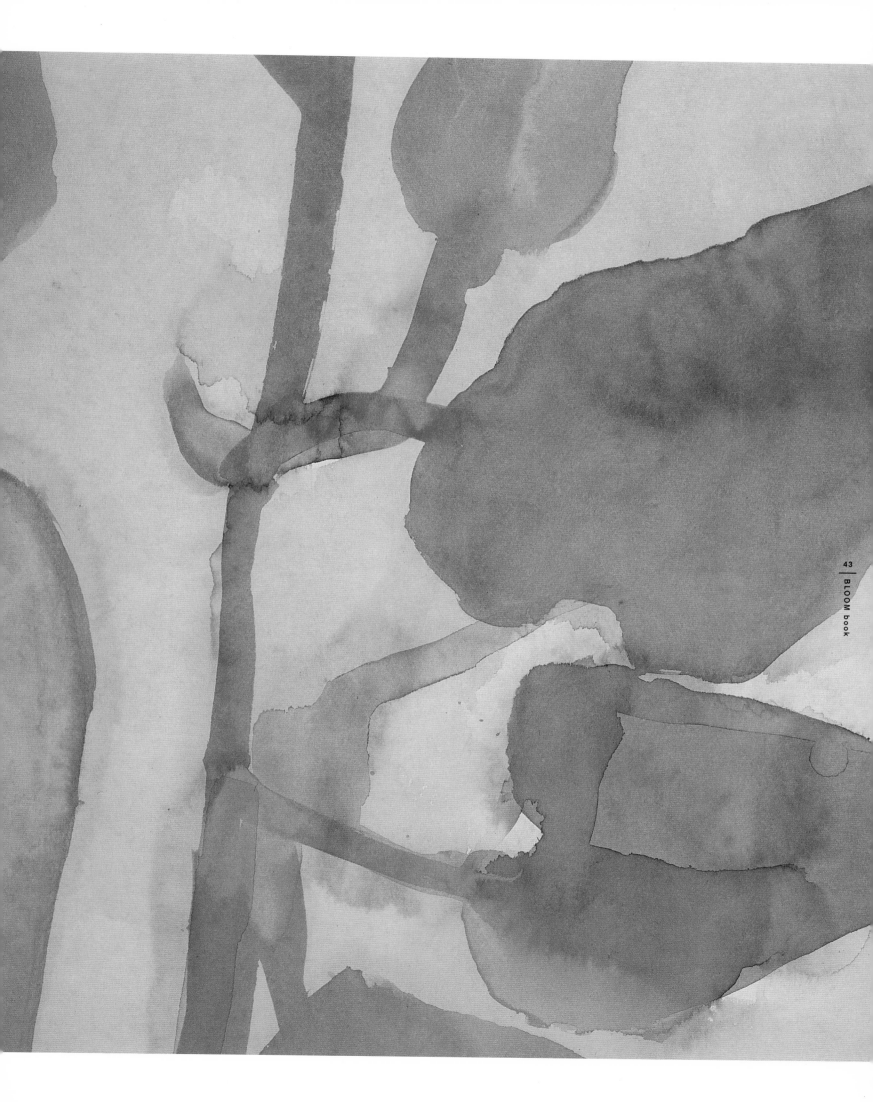

We are entering an era in which leaves are commanding as much attention as flowers. We study them for their graphic and sculptural forms, their textures, their colours and scents. Some leaves look like works of art, like Matisse's cut-outs. Others inspire us to compose all-leaf bouquets, and still others prompt us to purchase a plant regardless of its flowers, such as the waxy dark green of gardenia leaves or the feathery fronds of wisteria leaves. We relish the patterned leaves of the *Begonia rex,* and stroke the furry surface of the *Kalanchoe beharensis* as if it were a domestic animal. We stand in awe of the enormous *Victoria amazonica* leaves which grow up to 2 metres in diameter, or we grow in our garden the 1 metre-wide leaves of the *Gunnera manicata*—both of which take leaf-mania to giant proportions.

Indeed, green is a force to be reckoned with. We speak of green-backs in money, Green Berets in the armed forces, green parties in politics and the green movement in ecology. Green can be militant, as army uniforms often attest, but it is also the colour of camouflage, of blending in and getting along with one's environment. Green is generally pacific—the shade of neutrality. Green is equilibrium. Green is peace. And we must remember that green means Go: above all, it reflects a positive outlook on life. ■

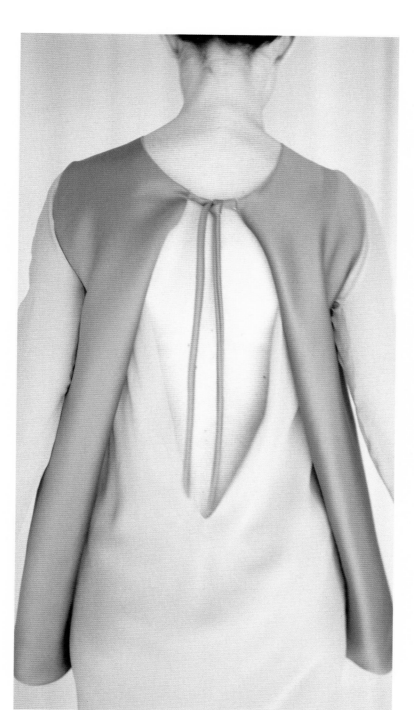

Notes

[1] **View in color magazine**
issue 9
1996

[2] **ibid**

[3] **Birren**, Faber
Color Psychology and Color Therapy
Citadel Press
Secacus, New Jersey, 1950

[4] **Nemitz**, Barbara
Transplant, Living Vegatation in Contemporary Art
Hatje Cantz, Ostfildern-Ruit

[5] **Pelt**, Jean-Marie
Les langages secrets de la nature, le communication chez les animaux et les plantes
Fayard, Paris, 1996

Other sources

Vitale Thomas, Alice
Leaves in Myth, Magic and Medicine
Stewart, Tabori & Chang
New York, 1997

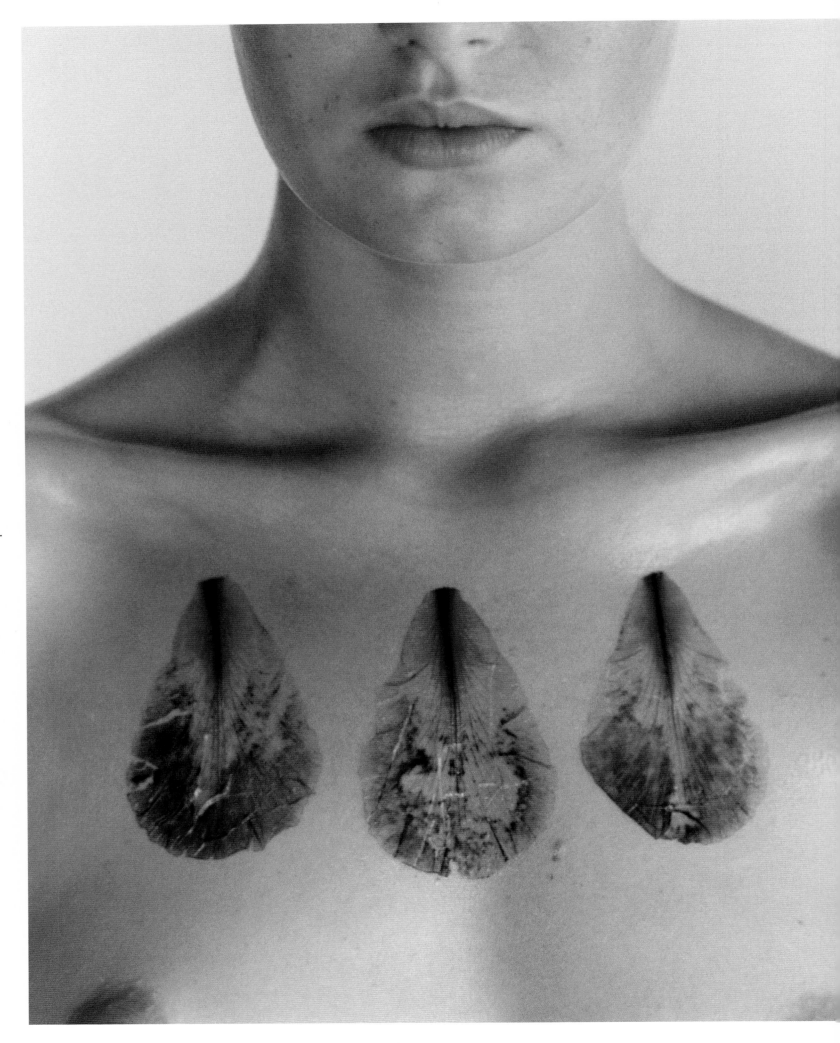

the beauty of **n a t u r e**

and botanical well-being

Beauty has been known to change the course of history, to modify destiny and to disrupt existing order. But most of the time beauty is to be found in small events, like a hidden notion. A thing of beauty is often ephemeral: a flower before wilting, a petal fallen from a tree, a fruit ready to be picked, the scent of summer's end. Beauty is there in the moment, ready to be captured in a photo, in an essence, in a fragrance.

Beauty is often aided by horticulture, where age-old recipes lay waiting to be rediscovered. Great grandmothers knew when to drink camomile, when to eat dandelion greens, where to apply cloves and how to burn eucalyptus. They understood that honey, the elixir from the gods, was able to cure small illnesses and to bring moist beauty to hair, skin and eyes. Back when man and nature spoke a universal language, humans knew instinctively that walnuts were beneficial for the brain and that beans could cure the kidney. Voodoo masters and witch doctors have used roots, leaves, petals and pollens for centuries to cure or to procure a sense of well-being.

Slowly, society opens up once more to botanical remedies and concoctions, embracing extracts to be swallowed, salves to be applied and fumes to be inhaled. We consider that beauty can engender beauty, that a healthy plant can make a healthy body, that plant life sustains our lives. The ultimate experiences are tested, such as drinking roots, chewing stems, eating spores, preserving petals: the horticultural spa is on its way!

We so enjoy the beauty in the taste, texture, colour and fragrance of botanical matter that we naturally mimic these ingredients in our cosmetic palettes and luxury perfumes. We strive to encapsulate the essence of the flower in all its guises. Ultimately, the flower and the woman will become one, lending each other colour, tactility and scent, creating a mirror image of the other. Then beauty can be forever.

                                        - L.E.

Why didn't nature endow humans with exquisitely coloured feathers or gorgeous fur? Mother nature decidedly saved her uncompromising stylist's eye for species other than ours. We are also the only animal to worry about ageing, which is of course why powders, perfumes, beauty masks and balms have their origins rooted in antiquity. The balm, whose first ingredient was either raw or cooked apple pulp, was to become what we know today as beauty creme. In times past, our ancestors employed a vast array of plants for both healing and beauty purposes. Leaves, flowers, buds, roots, trees and bark were the constituents of any lotion, tint, astringent, scent or unguent used to enhance appeal and maintain good health.

Use of some flowers for beauty purposes was more widespread than others and their benefits have crossed millennia without losing any of their potency and appeal. The most obvious example is the rose, whose multiple charms, essence, extracts and virtues have made it one of mankind's most consummate beauty products. More than 4 000 years ago, Sumerians used rose oil as a basis for their rubdowns. Rose leaves contain a lot of tannins and, as a result, are an excellent astringent, good for the pores of the skin. Furthermore, essential rose oil has been appreciated for its anti-wrinkle action, since it regenerates skin tissue. Rosewood extract has similar properties and has the advantage of being considerably less expensive than rose oil. This latter's price, beating that of all other essential oils, can be better understood when one learns that it takes 60 000 roses to make just 30g of its essential oil. The true, thick and strongly scented rose essence seems to have been discovered by Mannucci, a renowned Italian doctor. During a stay in India, he found a narrative of the lavish Moghol wedding of Emperor Djahanguyr to a proud princess.

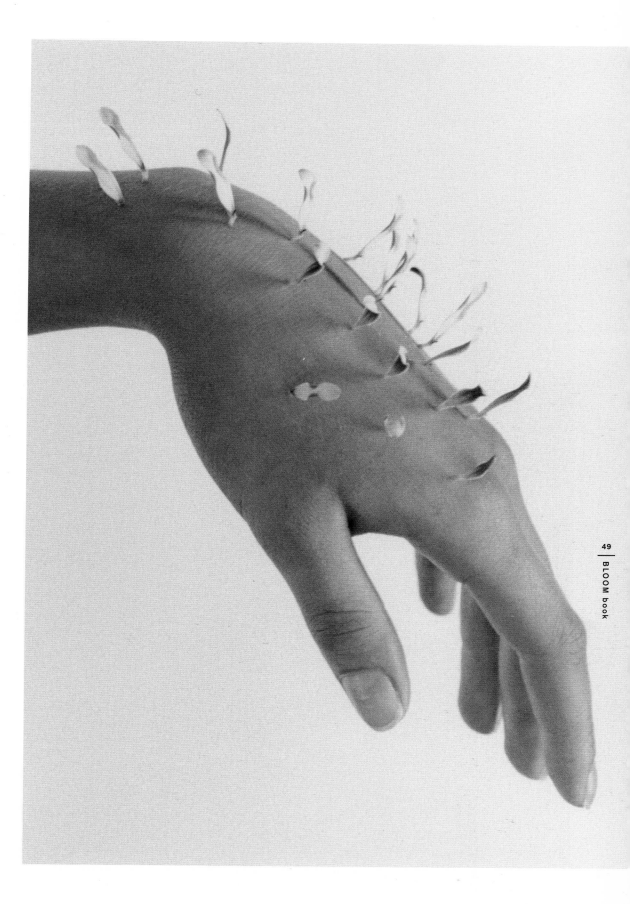

With flourish, and in a demonstration of utter luxury, the princess gave a sumptuous feast and apparently went so far as to have rose water circulate in the palace garden canals. As the Emperor walked with his bride at the canals' edge, he noticed foam floating on the water's surface. Intrigued, he had it removed in order to study it—to ultimately discover that it was a product of the rose's own substance. The entire court agreed that it was the most delicately scented oil imaginable. From that time on, attempts were made to reproduce this miracle of perfection that chance made available to an astute observer.[1]

Today's harsh, industrialized and ever more commercial society is a source of frequent aggressions. Products sold to help protect, cleanse and beautify can be the cause of many troubles. The irritating capacity of chemicals, stabilizers, moisturiser and shaving creams is well-known to dermatologists and can keep doctors' waiting rooms full of patients. Chemical products have the advantage of being easy to use and keep, whereas plant remedies need to be prepared, stored in a refrigerator and used rapidly before the plant decomposes. It takes a different kind of organization to be able to replace mass-produced beauty products by a range of plant preparations. Although not always—some plants and fruits, like the lemon, the aloe leaf, the simple potato or cucumber, can easily be helpful. An aloe leaf plucked fresh from the garden and placed on sun-burned skin will sooth the sore epidermis.

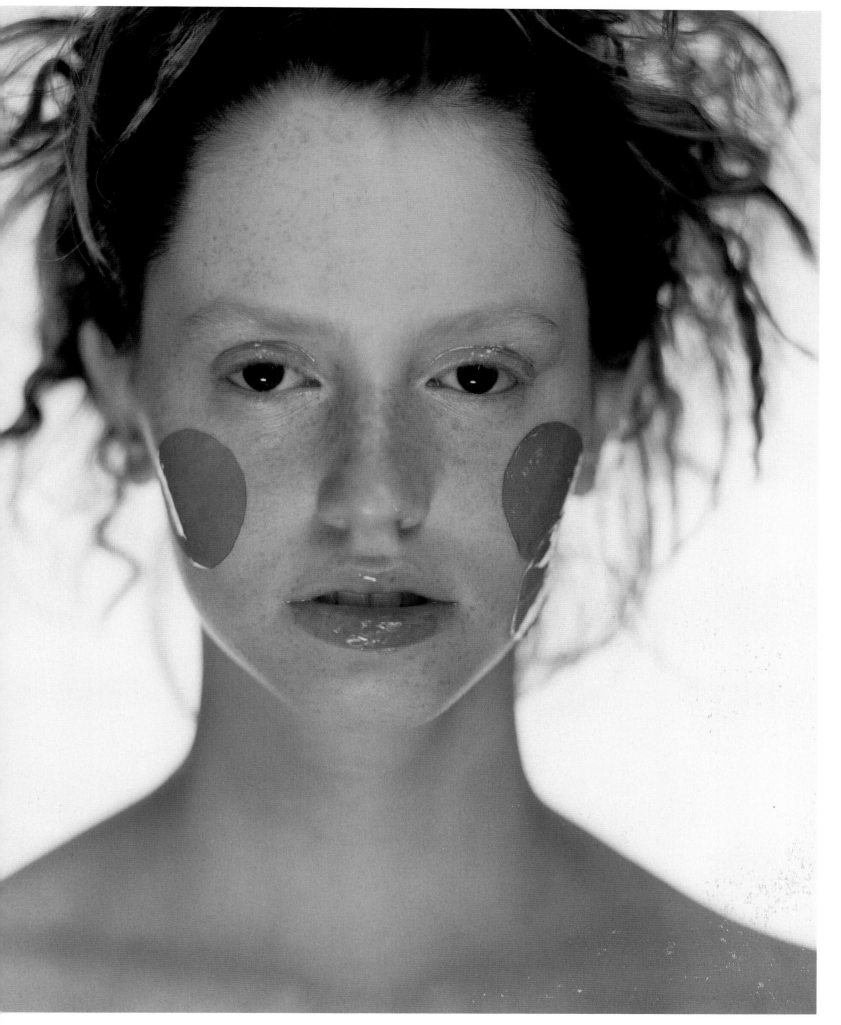

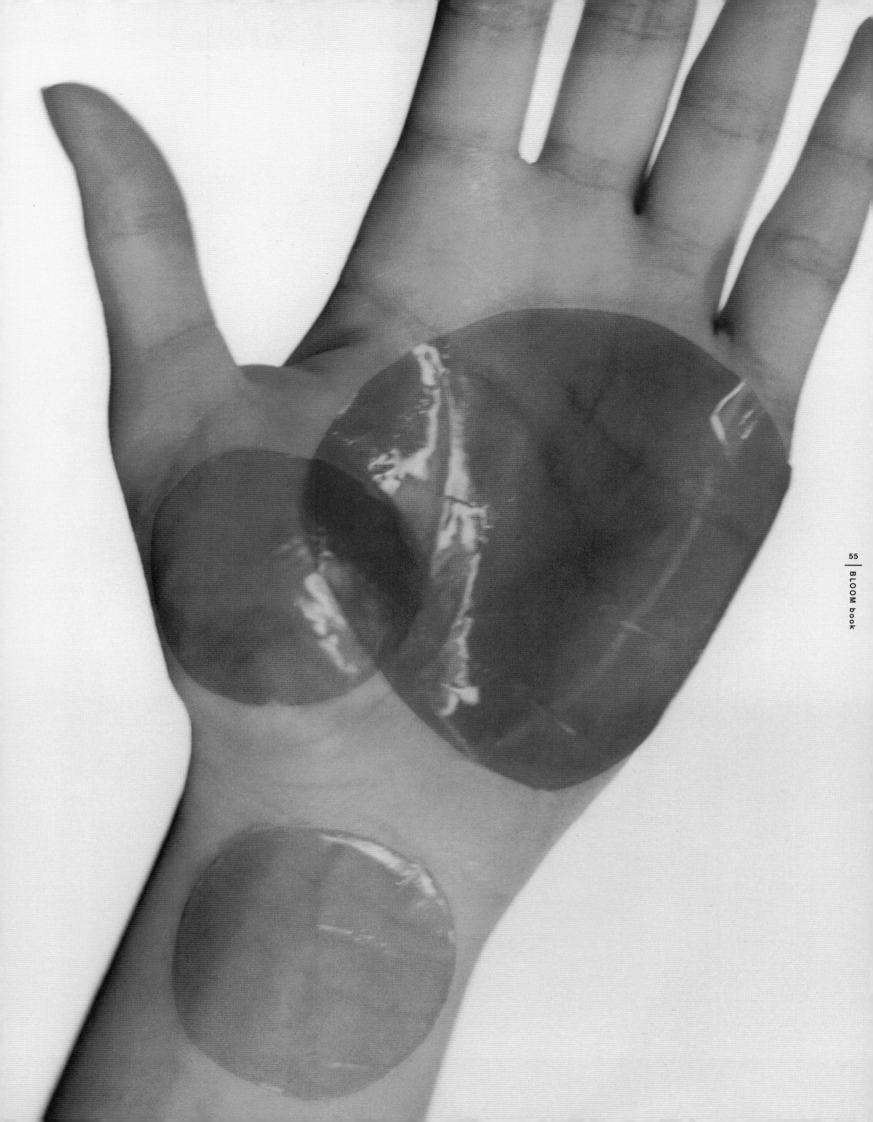

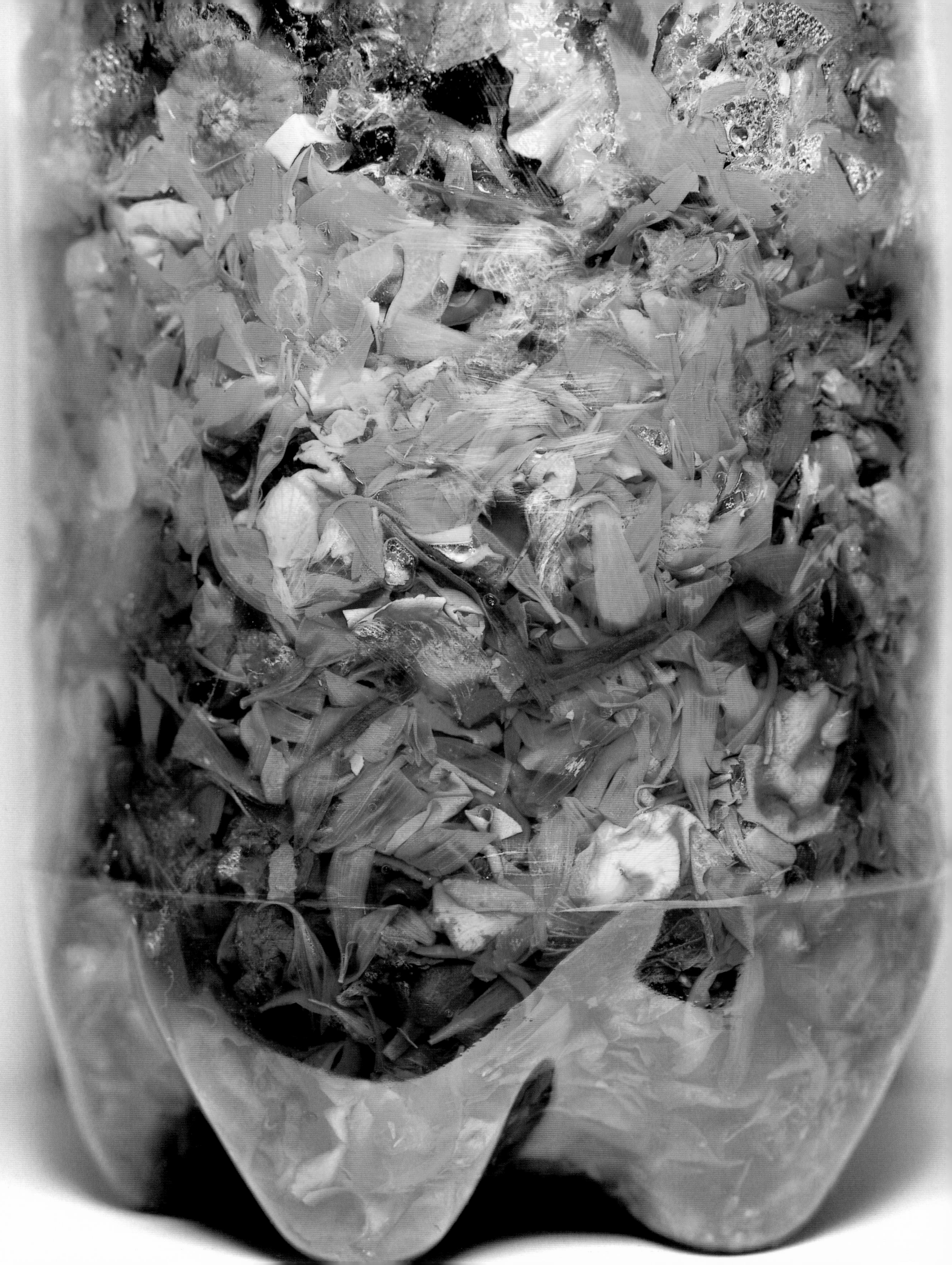

By grating a potato or slicing a cucumber, one immediately obtains a soothing face mask. Nettles, to be picked of course with care, are also plants with a wide scope of application. As an infusion, pouring a cup of boiling water on one to three teaspoons of the dried herb, nettle is an excellent astringent which strengthens the whole body.

It is best to simply allow nature's own structures to dictate beauty and logic. The mud shampoo *rassoul*, used diluted in a little warm water by the women of North Africa and which leaves hair clean and very silky, comes to mind. Honey gives off and absorbs moisture from the atmosphere, a quality which makes it highly suitable for facial masks, shampoos and other bodily pleasures. Soap is a thing of beauty, too. Unctuous like magnolias or smooth like camellias with fleshy textures and scents reminiscent of days gone by, authentic soaps are tactile treasures in themselves.

The most evident floral elixir is perfume. Whether gleaned from the process of *enfleurage* using animal fat, distilled with boiling water or extracted with a volatile solvent, floral essences contain all the power of their original blossoms. Indeed, one gram of jasmine absolute contains the energy of the 8 000 blossoms that were hand-picked for its creation. Perfumes are the subject of myriad poems and books, but just as captivating are the *parfums à boire* developed by Serge Calvez at the Petrossian restaurant in Paris. After his initiation into the art of infusing flowers, barks, spices and other natural elements in the Spice Islands, Calvez today distills perfumed drinking potions at the diner's table towards the end of a fine meal. Concocted to complement the many flavours of a full-course repast, these digestive drinks bloom on the tongue, such as the jewel-red 'Tears of the Nile', composed around Egyptian hibiscus, which cleanses the palate of sugar. A subtle alchemy of flavour that is magic for the mouth.

Flowers, in all their intricacy, are vectors of beauty. Observing them and their ephemeral lives is a splendid lesson in comeliness, with aroma and sensuality playing a major role. Some flowers, like daisies, are just good-humored and playful, smiling at the world with unabashed simplicity, cheerful and happy to be pretty and fresh. Others are like courtesans, sometimes more difficult to apprehend, slowly unfolding their petals, *dolcemente,* on a balmy summer's evening, seemingly lost in their own intimate thoughts.

The notion of *inner beauty* can apply just as well, indeed sometimes even more, to flowers than to humans. One wonders at their hues, the intricacy of their stamen and pistils and petal shapes so delicate that they seem worked in the finest enamel, shaped by a master craftsman. Their depths hide organic treasures, so aesthetically perfect that they even appear synthetic, or capable of upstaging the most precious of jewels. Their multiple layers also incite and promote new thoughts and directions regarding couture and cosmetics, jewels and plastics, packaging and porcelain. These flowers and their wondrous volumes, colors and textures hold design secrets that unfold before our eyes.

Of the flower's many companions, one of the most exquisite is dew, whose virtues have been venerated and extolled by man since time immemorial. Born of the night's dampness and condensed as if by magic, dew's diaphanous pearls shine brightly in the early morning light on flowers seemingly drunk with its essence. Its beauty is as pleasant a sight as its flower-charged moisture is refreshing. The idea of appropriating dew to embellish our complexions is appealing, like a liqueur for the skin.

We can use some of the flower's attributes, like its hues and textures, for our own color codes and dressing. Plants like nettle, hemp, linen and cotton provide a vegetal look. On the other hand, a fine silk or nylon netting knit worn over the naked body could create the spectacular image of an elusive blossom. By the same token, one could place flowers in rounded, epidermic vases whose shapes would be reminiscent of an exotic odalisque's generous forms. Each silhouette showing off, in coquettish fashion, the other's attributes. . . .

And so it goes with beauty. Nature's shapes, volumes, shades and scents surround and condition our lives; we are not always aware of them and do not always have the good sense to obey her laws and structures but, when we have the presence of mind to do so, we are inevitably gratified. It is then that one realizes to what extent nature's multiple facets are an inexhaustible source of inspiration. One should never underestimate the vital importance of aesthetics . . . of beauty for beauty's sake. It's a rare commodity, one which makes life ever so much more exciting and interesting, lifting existence, with a dash of color, beyond the everyday. ∎

Notes

[1] **Caron Lambert**, Alice
Le Goût de la Rose
Editions du HuitièmeJour
Paris, 2000

Other sources

De la Tour, Charlotte
Le Language des Fleurs
Garnier Frères
Paris, 1845

Irvine, Susan
Perfume
Haldane-Mason Books
London, 1996

an eye for composition

and the creative consumer

Contemplate an ordinary flower in a unique vessel or some exotic leaves in a vintage milk jar; imagine sturdy indigenous species blended with fragile Victorian flowers, an encounter of dried seed-pods with exuberant blooms. Combining and contrasting and playing with living matter, mastering all elements, making them sing together while enhancing each other's qualities: high and low, heavy and light, bourgeois and eccentric, cultured and natural, even real and fake!

This is a story of creating bouquets and centrepieces and showstoppers to surprise and–why not–to disconcert all senses. Built up as a fragrance, organised like a symphony or assembled as a recipe, all these studies introduce us to the instinctive power of creativity.

Sure of his own taste and desires, the creative consumer will invent personal ways to mix herbs with flowers, to assemble vegetables with foliage or to contrast driftwood with feathery grasses. The sky is the limit of his imagination, in the composition of a new garden, in the laying out of a blooming pond or in the architecture of a flowering pergola.

Furthermore, this new creative approach makes us collectors of glasswork and ceramics, baskets and beyond; to mix and dis-match shapes and sizes or volumes of vessels to make a family of objects, each containing its own botanical element.

Composing with over- and undersized vases, rough and glazed pottery, transparent and opaque glass, industrial and artisanal design–like plastic with ceramic matter–we play games of free association.

Creating these contemporary still-lifes with a budding talent for composition leads us to become Sunday artists everyday, once in awhile and only for a minute. . . .

– L.E.

When imagining an ideal bouquet of flowers, the Flemish still-life master-paintings of the late 15th century often come to mind. Lavish arrangements of lush yet highly composed blossoms—perfectly formed peonies, exotic flamed tulips, fritillaries, snowdrops and columbine—are extremely dense, yet each flower is depicted in its individual splendour, and often from different perspectives. The strength of these compositions arises not only from their pictorial beauty, but also from their symbolic factor. During this period, floral compositions began to replace the Biblical themes of the previous centuries, yet the presence of flowers and natural elements still evoked the divine. Every detail could be interpreted as a religious statement: a white lily representing the purity of the Virgin Mary, a butterfly embodining the Resurrection. At a time when the bourgeoisie were amassing fortunes and acquiring access to luxury, these flower paintings and their *vanitas* symbolism reminded patrons of the ephemeral nature of earthly life and possessions. Still other drawings were made for pharmaceutical study; thus, plants and bouquets could be considered healing in both the spiritual and medical senses.[1] Indeed, the generous yet delicate arrangements seem illuminated from within, a vibrant metaphor of life itself.

Later on, in the 17th century, paintings known as 'flower pieces' were a main source of decoration in homes. Not only was an original painting of a bulb flower often cheaper than the flower itself, but people could also appreciate the beauty of the painted flowers all year long. Though they seem quintessentially natural, the artists were not always concerned with depicting nature realistically, as they portrayed bouquets of flowers not in season together, and placed flowers with short stems at the outside edges of enormous arrangements where it would have been impossible for them to reach the water in the vase.

Furthermore, the most expensive flowers, such as tulips and irises, were usually painted at the tops of bouquets even though they were generally the heaviest of the bunch and would have weighed down the rest of the arrangement. Thus, these idealised bouquets often reflected values rather than reality.

During Victorian and Edwardian times, the 'language of flowers' became more moral and social than religious in theme, with red roses standing for true love and camellias for admiration, and floral compositions became more complicated as well, going far beyond bouquets. Now masses of flowers were a staple in country and city estates in order to supply the blossoms needed for frequent entertaining. Flowers were in such demand that hothouses were a necessity for the wealthy, whose gardeners had to produce enough blooms to create the amazing table decorations of the day. At this time, arrangements were essentially composed of only one type of flower, to show that the hosts had a sizeable greenhouse and production. More than two different kinds of flowers in a bouquet was considered vulgar or a sign of relative poverty. Ladies spent hours each day preparing flowers for every room, planning elaborate decorations for the many luncheons and dinners they hosted. At one point, the floral compositions reached absolute excess, as an 1878 letter from a furious socialite to the English magazine *Garden* attests: 'No longer is it possible to dine in comfort with abundance of good talk to aid digestion, for now there are rocks, lakes, streams, waterfalls, ponds, glaciers, dense masses of foliage and flowers, tanks of moss, zinc dishes and glass dishes innumerable—all piled on the table to swamp the dinner and prevent the diners from either seeing each other, or their dinner, or indeed, anything save the decorations.'[2] A point certain overzealous florists would still do well to heed today. . . .

At the other end of extremes is ikebana, the philosophy of flower arranging which has been practised in Japan in various forms since the 7th century. The goal of ikebana is to recreate the balance of nature, and the arrangement should look as if it had simply grown that way. More recent schools of ikebana incorporate new materials with flowers, such as roots, wood and metal, though the goal remains the same: one should get the impression that the composition was taken straight from nature before being placed in the *tokonoma*, a special alcove present in all traditional homes, for the purpose of greeting guests with an ikebana composition and a calligraphy-painted message of the season.

Whatever the philosophy, a successful floral composition is one that takes into consideration the flowers themselves.

Not to torture mowers into static architecture, but to listen to them and let their small voices be heard above the voice of the arranger.

Otherwise, there are no rules: mix wild flowers with garden flowers, exotic blooms with domestic blossoms, real flowers with plastic ones, spring flowers with autumn ones. An arrangement of ranunculus, iris and anigozanthos is a feast of matter and light while an association of an aloe with irises invites contemplation. Fruits and vegetables can be part of the tableau—especially since they were once grouped with flowers and plants in the general category of 'herbs'— and demonstrate our desire to create gorgeous still-lifes with our fresh produce, keeping it on display instead of storing it in the refrigerator.

Containers, vases and vessels also play an important role in the general picture.

The Japanese say that 'choosing the vase is already creating part of the bouquet.'³ Sometimes these vessels complement the flowers, such as felt and latex vases that mirror the elastic yet velvety texture of sage and lavender. Porous white ceramics can also mimic the texture of celery root, which then becomes itself part of the sculptural arrangement. Kitchen gardens, with their fresh herbs and roots, are making a comeback and the medieval 'Garden of Simples' (*Jardin des Simples)* that incorporated aromatic and medicinal plants, shows us today how to live an essential, yet sensual life. Mixing herbs with flowers and fruit in compositions may now lack the allegory of masterpiece paintings, yet the vision is still there, calling us to find strength and healing in nature.

Other containers might recall the textures and shapes of the flower's indigenous country. For example, old landmasses like Australia breed tough-looking plants that call for rustic vessels, in the way an ostrich egg or carved root vase enhances the ancient aspect of banksia flowers. A coffee pot can bring out the homeliness of a European garden bouquet while exquisite Oriental pottery is the perfect setting for a branch of cherry blossoms.

We can also learn from other civilisations' original ways to compose flowers. Take for example the Brokpa people, who live in the remote Da valley located between Pakistan and India, 3100 metres above sea-level, up where the air turns blue and all nature takes on an almost vibrant aura.

Historically merchants along this part of the Silk Road, the Brokpa are now farmers, and they grow not only the vegetables they need to eat, but also cultivate flowers for pure pleasure. Both Buddhists and Animists, the Brokpa have a strong respect for nature, and even make it part of the composition of their everyday attire. Women and men embellish their hats with fresh and dried flowers, bringing a sense of festivity to quotidian activities, whether cooking or labouring in the fields. Like a bouquet for the body, the blossoms have both a personal and a physical relationship with the wearer.

Such personal compositions, based on intuition, often defy any sort of rules or constraints. Gaugin, who escaped to Tahiti to be in closer contact with instinctive nature, exclaimed that he was 'seeking to express the harmony between human life and that of animals and plants in compositions in which I allowed the deep voice of the earth to play an important part.'[4] As such, his paintings reflect a harmony of form and colour that is almost tangible. Another painter, Alexej Jawlensky, claimed, 'I do not want to spread myself out on the surface, but to delve into the depths.'[5] In turning this inspiration the other way around, we can also conceive arrangements loosely inspired by paintings or other art forms, with compositions of colour, texture and shape that attempt to delve deep into a common perception of nature.

Apart from flower arranging, one of the most obvious applied compositions of nature is cuisine. Taking the animal and vegetal to new heights, we have begun cooking with flowers. A sprinkling of bright orange nasturtiums in a salad, zucchini-blossom beignets and a rose sorbet for dessert are no longer rare delicacies. (To prepare them oneself, be careful to choose only home-grown flowers that have never been treated with pesticides.) However, to cook flowers is an entirely new business. The noted flower researcher and *gastronome* Alice Caron Lambert has spent years developing floral recipes in her native France, some of the most surprising of which are soups. Cream of broccoli with mimosa, cream of primrose, chrysanthemum soup with saffron croutons, and shrimp bouillon with wild pansies and violets are composed with the same nutritional and gourmet care as a still life.

On another level of taste, fashion also takes its inspiration from flowers, developing materials that might evoke the layers of a carnation or the froth of a spider chrysanthemum.

Christian Lacroix, the French designer with a flower fetish, once teamed up with florist Henri Moulié to create a couture show based on colourful carnations. Coco Chanel made the camellia her emblem and Kenzo has made floral prints a major part of his life's work. We can dress ourselves as if we were a bouquet, with pants or skirt as vase and stem, bodice or wrap, shirt or vest, bracelets, hat and accessories as the corollas, and our sexy selves as the central pistil.

Whether partaking of floral arrangements with our eyes, noses, fingertips, mouths or our entire bodies, we take pleasure in composing our surroundings with the eye of a master, beholding beauty exactly as we see it. ■

Notes

[1] **Schneider**, Norbert
"The Early Floral Still Life"
In *The Art of the Flower*
Edition Stemmle
Zürich, 1996

[2] **Blacker**, Mary Rose
Flora Domestica
The National Trust
London, 2000

[3] **Sollers**, Philippe
"Fleurs du Temps"
In *L'Ikebana*
Martine Clémént
Editions Denoël, 1997

[4] **Chipp**, Herschel B.
Theories of Modern Art
University of California Press
Berkeley and Los Angeles, 1968

[5] *Jawlensky*
Exhibition Catalogue
Musée-Galerie de la Seita,
Paris, 2000

a look at **volume**

and the sculptural potential of plants

For centuries, society has seen flowers and plants as frivolous single items in need to be bound in a bouquet or regrouped on a windowsill in order to become interesting. Little nothings to be combined to create a larger whole. Flowers belonged to a family of flowers, foliage belonged to an army of plants. The art of flower and garden arrangement spread through all cultures and is fondly remembered in Indian miniatures, Japanese engravings, and Flemish paintings. Still blooming today.

Yet another look at nature is being discovered, drastically changing how we perceive flowers, the way we look at leaves, the manner in which we contemplate plants. A way in which we scrutinise nature in a precise and discerning manner, discovering a style in form and volume. We find that nature has designed its components like a master potter, a driven sculptor, an abstract painter, a fashion designer. Nature has conceived its elements with a focus on material and colour to be used in favour of form to enhance and to highlight shape, to make volume stand out.

Bright yellow gives meaning to the radiant aura of the sunflower and makes it into a vibrant manifesto of summer. Lacquered red surfaces help extreme, sharp shapes or exotic species stand out, to attract birds and butterflies. All shades of green define the inspirational forms of seed pods while duller hues of grey and green emphasise the spherical, other-worldly quality of the cactus family. X-rayed blossoms give us a new eye with which to discover botanicals: close-ups of surreal beauty.

The architecture of a plant, the vaults of a flower, the rhythm of a leaf, the construction of a fruit all inspire us to invent containers, to design staircases and to develop clothes. Volume lends horticulture its cultural component.

- L.E.

o enter into our studies of volume, we prefer to contemplate a single, individual flower or form, to look at it with the eyes of an artist, appraising its shape, its density, its weight, texture, colour and pattern. Buying flowers can be like buying art, a monumental decision even if they last just a moment in our lives. And every flower, every plant has its own intrinsic beauty.

Close study of flowers can make one passionate, and many growers, small or large, concentrate on propagating only one type of flower or plant alone. André Eve, considered by many to be the guru of roses, grows 500 different species, both new hybrids of his own creation and old roses, in his small garden near Pithiviers, France. Sharon and Neville Trickett, who created the revolutionary plant store Saint Verde in the hills outside Durban, South Africa, built their store concept around a garden of echeverias, cacti and succulents. Creating their garden from a sculptural point of view, they carefully chose the plants for their volume and shape, explaining, 'We want to make the gardening dynamic in people's lives more important, to help people to see that there is a new way to look at gardens and flowers and rooms.'

For larger growers, cultivating flowers in volume is a true industry. In Holland, one of the key flower-production countries of the world, flowers are commodities with their own auction market, the Bloemen-veiling, based in Aalsmeer. Dutch flower production represented 42 percent of Holland's net balance of agricultural trade in 1999[1], which, in practical terms, can be translated into 12 billion cut flowers and 665 million green and flowering plants.

Unlike most other industries, the flower trade reflects not only a love of trading itself, but also of blooms. From 1634 to 1637 in Holland, a particular time referred to as 'Tulipomania', the speculation on tulip bulbs reached an all-time high, with fortunes made and lost overnight, and some individual bulbs selling for as much as the price of a house. Tulips even had their own standard of weight, the *azen,* which reflected the bulb's weight at planting time.[2]

Today, the Dutch export about two billion tulip bulbs per year, with another billion for internal markets. About three-quarters of the total Dutch flower production is exported, which still leaves a great deal for internal consumption. And the Dutch love flowers. According to Jan Dippell, a master florist based in Amsterdam, 'The Dutch bill of rights guarantees four basic necessities that people cannot live without: water, electricity, shelter, and plants and flowers. Flowers are not considered a luxury, but a necessity. At local markets, people often arrive early to wait for the flowers and plants to arrive—they buy flowers before they buy food!'[3] Flowers are a pleasure we can, and should, enjoy every day.

No one has yet starved in order to purchase flowers (and indeed, in an interesting turn of events, the Dutch resorted to eating tulip bulbs in the darkest hours of World War II) but their contemplation is considered important as nourishment for the soul. To observe the head of a sunflower as it turns toward the sun, ripens and droops with the weight of its rich seeds, is to understand the process of life itself. To partake of the energy of the dahlia, with its finely curled petals and saturated colours, is to receive a jolt of joy. When we move in closer we see an entirely new world open to us. Penetrated by X-ray light, flowers lose their coyness and show their secret linings without reserve.

32
usa

GEORGIA O'KEEFFE

1996

Suddenly, we find ourselves contemplating the graphic and sculptural potential of a single petal or an entire cluster of florets.

By observing the flower in its own right and by taking inspiration from it, we can derive new studies of shapes in vessels. Many times, the ultimate vase is one that reflects the volume of the flowers themselves. Other times, we prefer the generous and varied shapes of the gourd, the ripe elegance of the bulb, the pregnant promise of the pod, the slender slope of the stem. We would like the container to be as natural in its form as in its contents.

Flowers as a study in volume have been part of the artistic psyche for centuries, in painting and, more recently, in photos. Studied by Karl Blossfeldt as inspiration for architecture or seized by Robert Mapplethorpe as an expression of utter sensuality, capturing the forms of the flower's anatomy is an attempt to achieve a template of perfection.

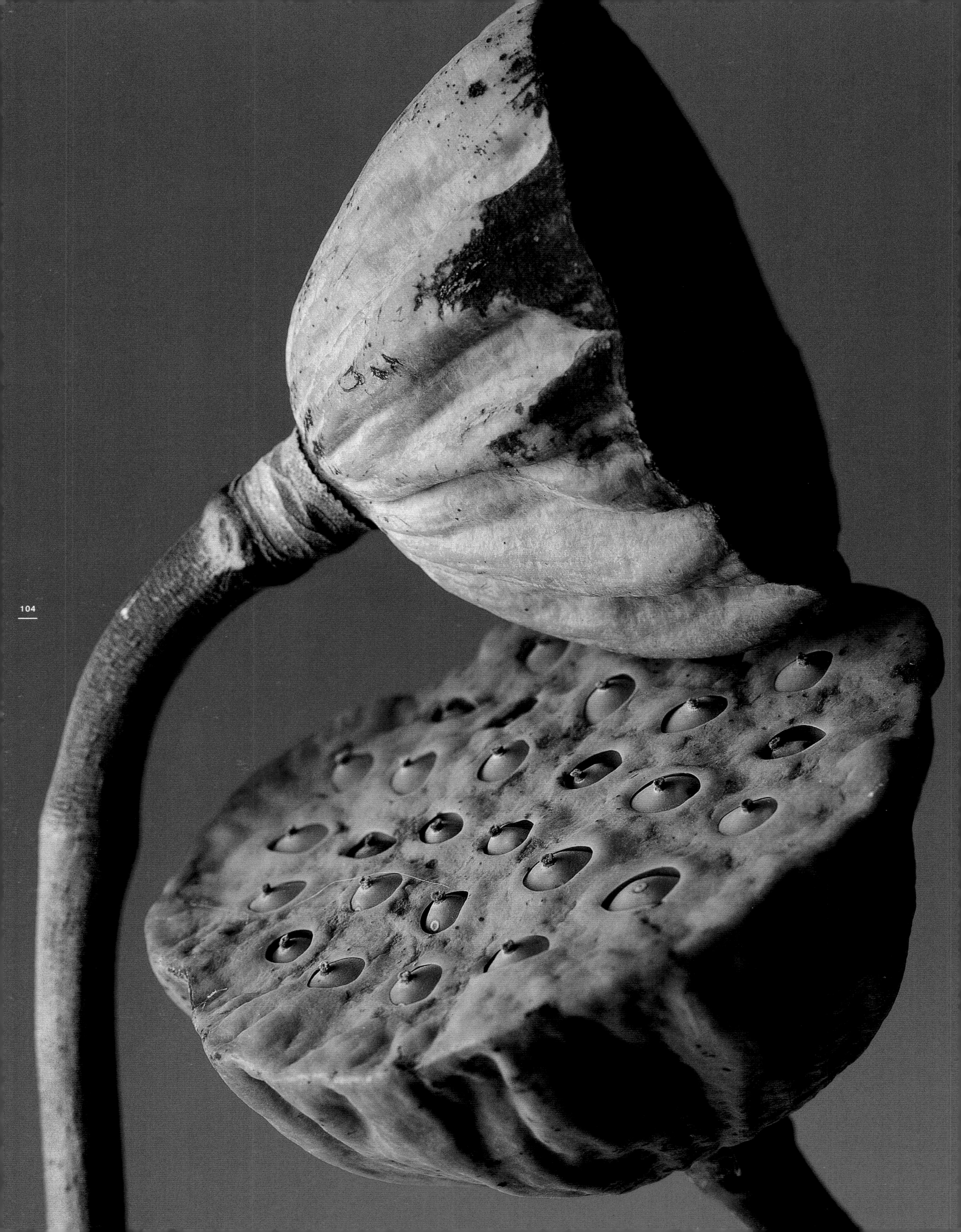

104

The French writer Georges Bataille stated in his essay 'The Language of Flowers' that 'It is interesting to observe, however, that if one says that flowers are beautiful, it is because they seem to *conform to what must be,* in other words they represent, as flowers, the human *ideal. . . .*'[4] Indeed, botanical nature sometimes seems so much more perfect than the often imperfect forms of human nature. Noted photographer Edward Weston once said that he felt more aroused when photographing the forms of cabbages and peppers than when photographing nudes.

Artist Georgia O'Keeffe took the volumes, colours and textures of flowers and enlarged them to monumental proportions so that, be they small paintings or enormous, two-metre canvases, the viewer is awe-struck by the sheer power of the flower. Painting them close up, in sensual, minute detail, O'Keeffe made us feel flowers in an entirely new way. She explained in 1946 in an interview in the New York Post: 'When you take a flower in your hand and really look at it, it's your world for the moment. I want to give that world to someone else. Most people in the city rush around so, they have not time to look at a flower. I want them to see it whether they want to or not'.[5]

The volumes of flowers and plants, when used as a means to an end, have the power to become an end in themselves, for they have a way of shining through creativity. Karl Blossfeldt did not begin photographing plants for their own sake, but instead for use as raw material for the drawing table, yet today his plant photos are considered masterpieces.

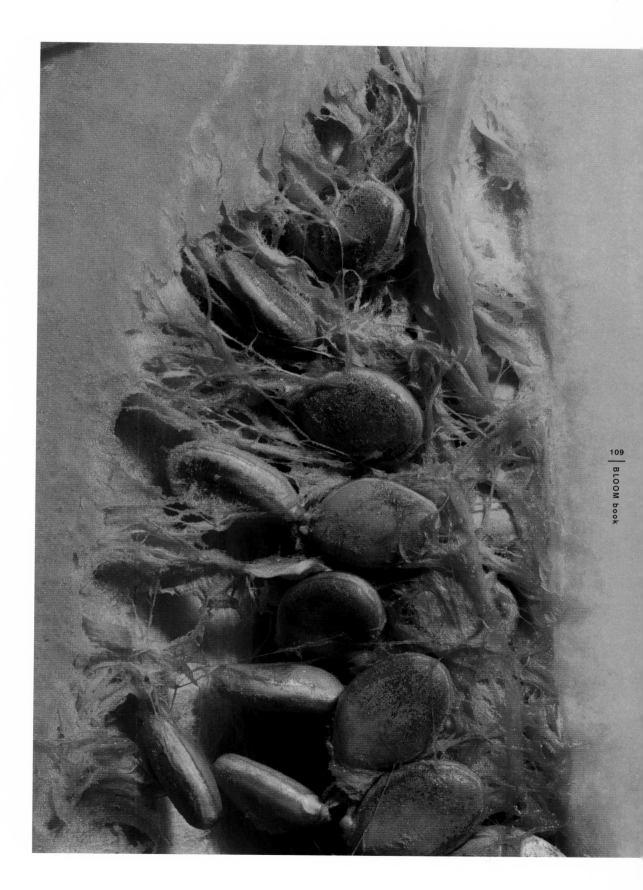

Flowers and plants are so much a part of our subconscious that sometimes they burst into being even if they were not part of the initial concept. The avant-garde Japanese designer Rei Kawakubo, in commenting on her seminal Winter 1997 collection of padded, wrapped and floral-printed clothes, claimed that 'The starting point was to have some fabric wrapped around you, so that you feel comfortable, and these abstract shapes ended up looking like a flower'. His compatriot, Junya Watanabe, created for his turn-of-the-century collection high-volume dresses and skirts in super-fine polyester that reminded one of the whorls and volutes of dahlias. Surrounded by voluminous layers of lightness wrapped around the models' bodies like enormous corollas, bursting with colour, the collection carried all the intensity of a natural phenomenon.

No matter what the final product, be it a jewel, a vase, a chair, a dress or even an entire building, the volumes of flowers and plants are embodied deep within our minds, spurring creativity and making much of our lives a celebration of floral shape and style. ∎

Notes

[1] Figures published by the Flower Council of Holland, 2001

[2] **Pavord**, Anna
The Tulip
Bloomsbury Publishing
New York and London, 1999

[3] **Bloom magazine**
issue 1
1998

[4] **Bataille**, Georges
'The Language of Flowers'
In *Visions of Excess,*
Selected Writings 1927-1939
University of Minnesota Press
Minneapolis, 1985

[5] **O'Keeffe**, Georgia
One Hundred Flowers
Ed. Nicholas Callaway
Callaway Editions, Inc.
1987

a quest for **freshness**

and the spring of spontaneity

Freshness is walking into your garden in the early morning to listen to an early bird chorus, to discover new blooms still covered with dew, to cut and collect a spontaneous bouquet. Freshness is travelling to the nearest farmers' market to buy wholesome food, healthy eggs, just-prepared cheeses and bunches of home-grown flowers, randomly tossed together and daringly multicoloured, wrapped in last Sunday's crossword puzzle. Freshness is collecting baby blooms in tiny vases or selecting giant spring blossoms, perched like butterflies on otherwise naked branches.

Freshness is about experiencing rather than contemplating. Freshness is like feeling young and free and playful. No rules, no regulations: everything is possible. Freshness is the future. An idea for survival and reversal, a way to reinvent our lives, a way to restructure our behaviour patterns, a way to break our daily routines. Freshness will influence our food, our cosmetics, our pharmaceuticals and our flowers. In the future, our fresh fridges will look distinctly different, housing all of these fresh elements and more—a reason why the refrigerator will become transparent, showing off its beautiful contents.

Freshness is a walk of life, walking away to re-think, discarding the old, embracing the new and the unpredictable, the simple and the straightforward, training the elastic of our brains. Freshness is rebounding and rejoicing like a metal spring, full of energy generated by the simplest of structures. Freshness is like running into the ocean or diving into a pond, baptised by the water gods.

Freshness is a new form of uncluttered and friendly design, a fashion of evident colours and square weaves in proven styles. Freshness represents the fusion of past and future. Freshness is more important than youth—it is the best way to grow old. Freshness is another way of looking at flowers, to locate them in their natural habitats, to gather them or just let them be. Freshness becomes a poem of everyday beauty, a nursery rhyme to celebrate life.

- L.E.

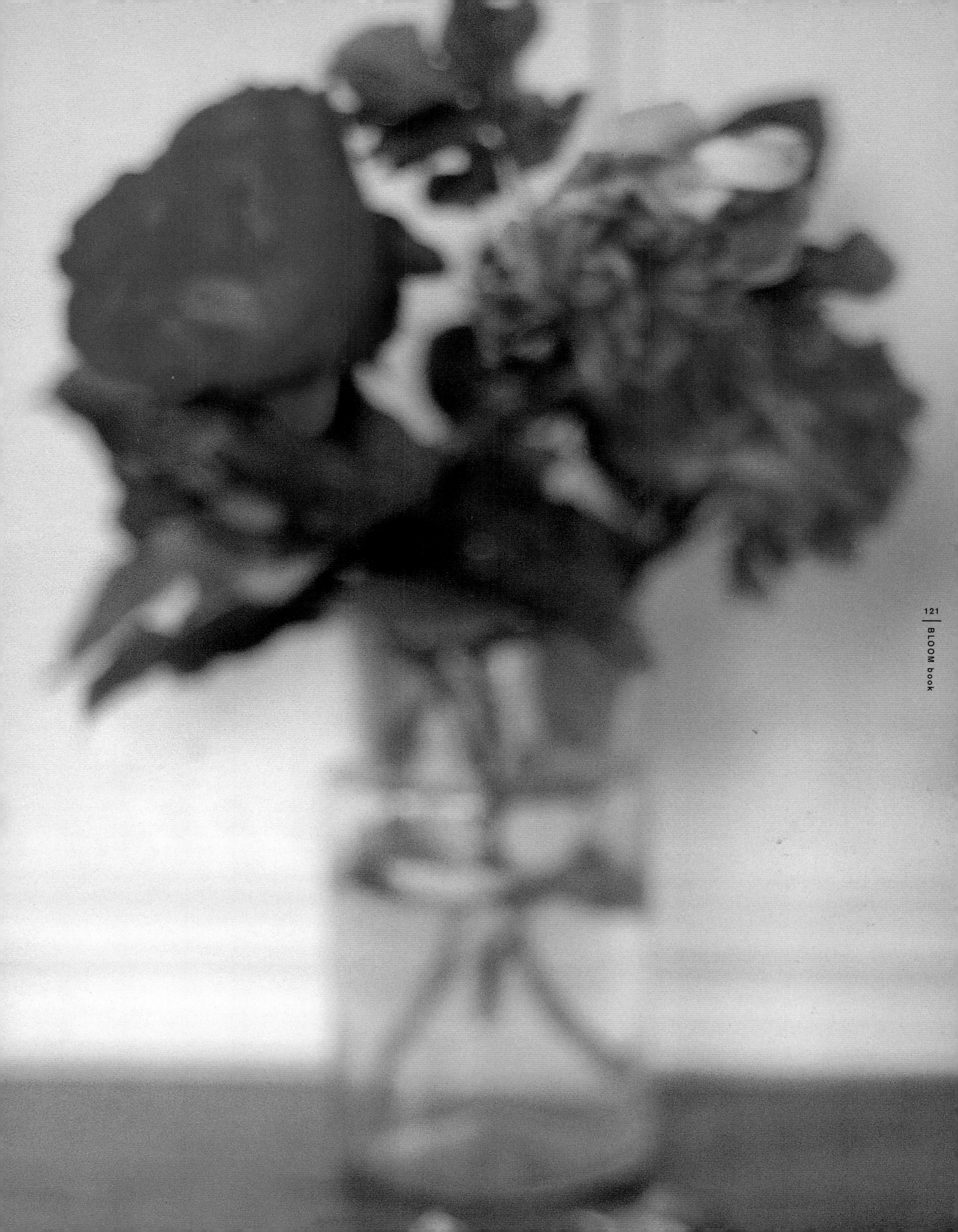

W hether purchased at the market, or plucked from the garden, woods or field, contemplating fresh flowers can be an emotional and profoundly satisfying experience. Colette, France's quintessential lover and observer of nature, who always had a very personal, often iconoclastic way of writing about what she sniffed and saw, spoke of the poetry in the '. . . disorder of corollas, the confusion of colours'[1] inherent to wild flowers. Her sense of smell was just as acute as her observations and played as well a role in determining freshness, or lack of it. Indeed, all senses are on alert where nature and its true scents are concerned. Colette had another witty outburst when she declared, 'But oh, how bottled scents deceive me! On the other hand, the wild onslaught which comes up, in summer, from chlorophyll torn by the storm, the iodine delivered at each low tide, the whiff belched out by the vegetable garden no longer capable of containing itself, by the compost heap where, together, black currant marc, torn fennel and old dahlia bulbs ferment, what incense for my independent and capricious olfactory nerves'.[2] Authentic odours, if not always fresh, have the merit of being true to nature.

Flowering plants abound naturally: there exist about 300 000 different species of them world-wide. We can be forgiven for our proclivity to consider them as purely decorative, as embellishments for the garden or cut for ephemeral pleasure inside the house. However, the natural function of flowers, aside from nourishing butterflies and bees, is one which is indispensable . . . the flower is the reproductive organ of its plant; the petals comprise an enticing and colourful wrap deep inside which bees can find necessary little deposits of nectar—and go about their sideline business of propagating flowers.

Polish writer Karel Capek exclaimed in his essay *Buds,* 'You must stand still, and then you will see open lips and furtive glances, tender fingers, and raised arms, the fragility of a baby, and the rebellious outburst of the will to live.' Indeed, it may seem to us that buds burst and flowers bloom just for the sake of being, just to exist and to drink up the sun and the dew, yet, like the stars they are, they shine and seduce to insure that they and their offspring will endure. Their freshness is thus also a way to appeal to others, be it a bee, a bird or a cultivating hand.

Luckily for us, most flowers can be found or grown in such an amount that we can benefit from this abundance, gathering cut flowers to brighten our homes, our clothes or our bodies. At the florists, we often find a breathtaking array of flowers, especially when the florist is in close contact with the passionate growers of each species, or when he or she also grows his own blossoms. Such a florist is Parisian Henri Moulié, who exclaims, 'We all have a vital need to be surrounded by flowers and plants, and my shop is like a garden that has just been cut and placed directly in the store.' A flower store in a downtown location can indeed be an oasis of freshness, a generous gathering of blooms.

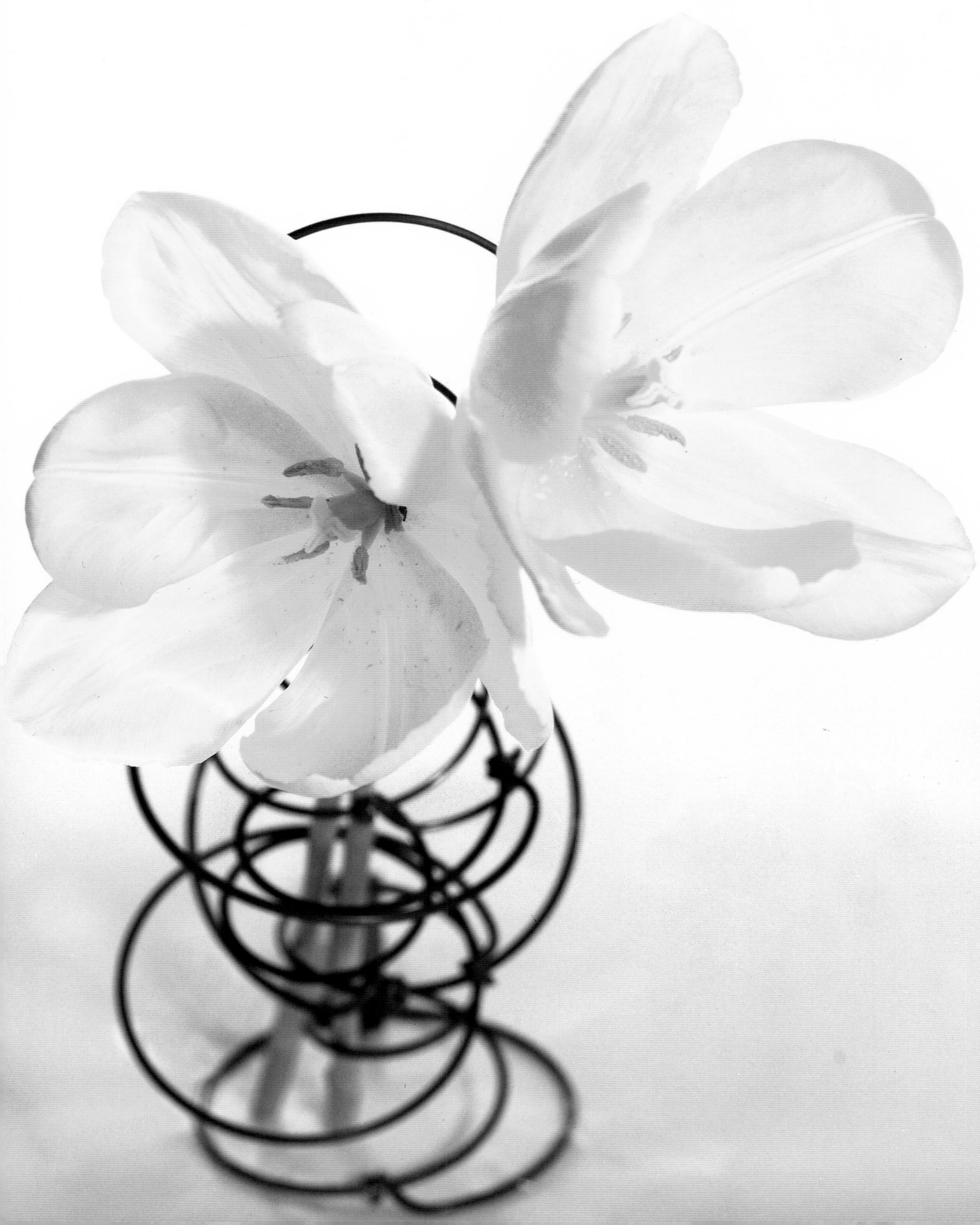

Yet another destination for all fresh flower-lovers is the country market. The ruddy cheeks of the flower vendor at a market in Normandy, the sun-tanned face of the local vegetable farmer at another market in the Basque country, the scents and colours of fresh foods and plants are a pure delight. Baskets of small red apples, long stalks of brightly-veined rhubarb, lettuce with dirt still clinging to its roots, freshly churned butter, feather-dusted eggs and fresh cheeses make up a still life that is completed by plastic buckets filled with a garden assortment of flowers, arranged into small bouquets by the gardener herself. Vendors in the countryside are often also growers of their vegetables and flowers and take pride in presenting them, extolling the virtues of the more uncommon ones. The open market accomplishes another purpose, which is one of conviviality. An exchange of news, comments regarding the produce, weather and various other subjects make market-going very pleasant and above all, very human. Flowers purchased in such a context are examples of authenticity. With uneven stems, insect-spotted leaves, pungent aromas and blossoms of imperfect perfection, these flowers have retained a naive and friendly freshness that simply cannot be mass-cultivated. Hydrangeas, cosmos, edible nasturtiums and roses are mixed together happily in eclectic, multi-coloured arrangements. Sometimes sprigs of mint and basil add an extra olfactory touch. Spontaneously cut, seemingly surprised to be there, market flowers are an urbanite's dream, to be simply placed in a drinking glass or in a jam jar, grandma's cut-glass vase or a bottle of water.

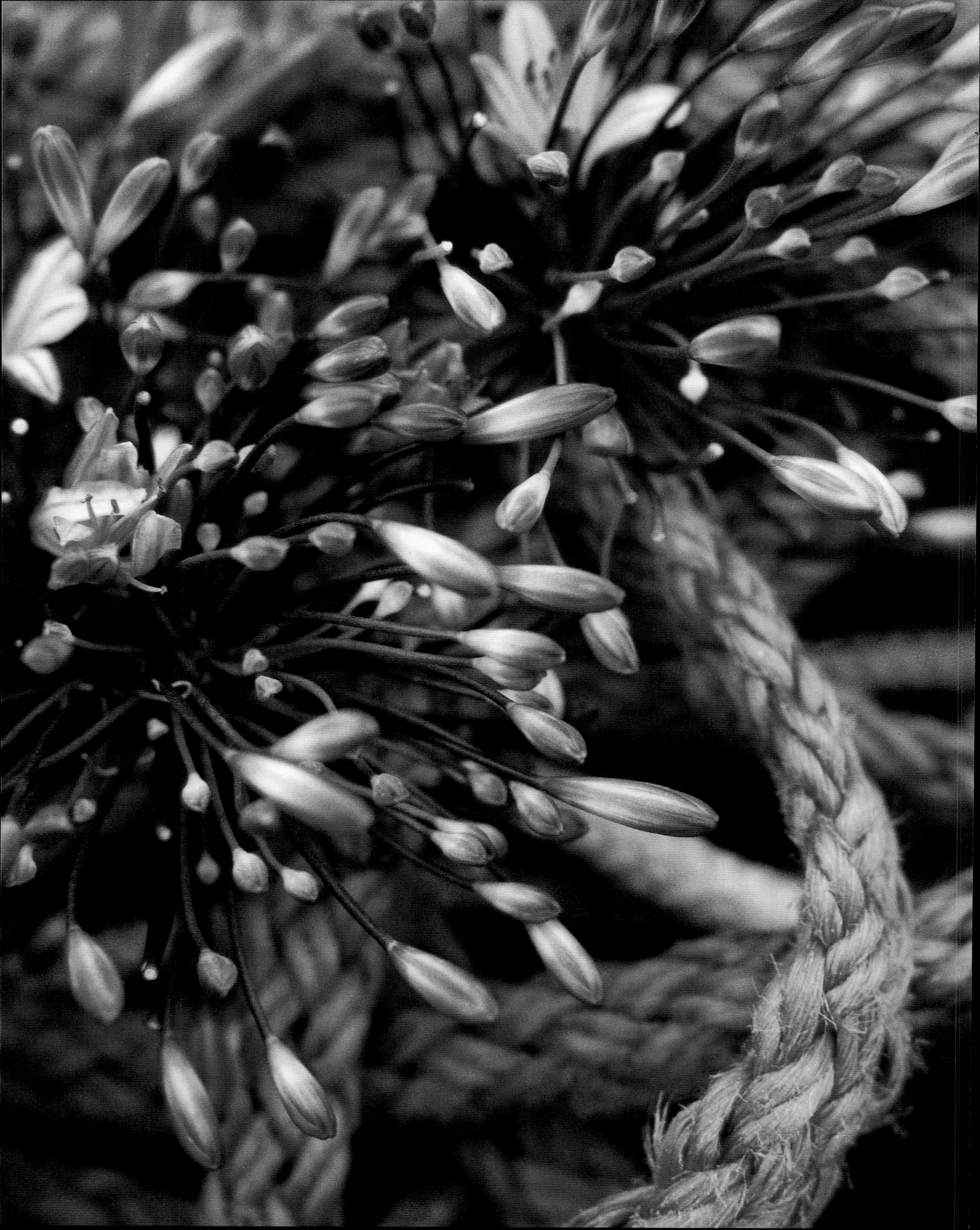

On the other hand, hothouse flowers, like babies conceived *in vitro,* are brought up in nurseries and require as much tender loving care, nourishment and fresh air as their two-legged counterparts. Carefully hybridised, scientifically gestated, despite their tender age they are the cooler, more professional members of the horticultural world. With their immaculate, long-lasting blossoms they offer the pictorial ideal of a flower, to be contemplated alone or incorporated into a magnificent still-life of picture-perfection. Though almost chilly in their flawlessness, the nature in hothouse hybrids still shines through.

It is a closeness with flowers that we seek; a way to incorporate their freshness into our lives. On the other end of the scale, we remember vividly the times in which we were confronted with the breathtaking vista of a field of wild flowers, whether a carpet of daisies or a hill of grasses peppered red with poppies, brightened yellow with buttercups, punctuated blue with bachelor's buttons. The very image of freedom, of endless days, of insouciance; we can remember picking handfuls of posies and taking them home, slightly wilted, to our mothers; we recollect gathering armfuls of multicoloured blossoms, still warm from the sun and teeming with life. We picked these flowers in relation to our own bodies, our hands and arms and laps, and to the possibilities we had to hold them until we offered them up to the civilising effect of a vase.

Whether grown in the garden, gathered wild in the fields, or selected straight from the hothouse, what a riot of colour, what ranges of hues flowers provide. Take, for example, shades of blue. We tend to associate them more with the sky and sea than with flower petals; and yet, some of the loveliest, most subtle shades are botanical blues, ranging from pale blue-grey to deepest mauve.

Delphiniums, hyacinths and hydrangeas are cases in point. We again refer to Colette, living in Paris and missing '. . . the frail daughter of the woods…the wild hyacinth . . . whose blooming forest blue, spontaneous and fragile, innumerable enough to give the illusion that (she was) next to a lake, or a flowering field of blue linen'. . . .[3] When such flowers are placed in settings among pebbles from a northern beach or on pieces of wood from an old fishing boat whose blue colours have been washed and worn incessantly by the tide, they supply a veritable breath of fresh sea air.

Flowers are not only colourful and coquette, they also symbolise various attributes like innocence, silence, voluptuousness, fecundity, grace and freshness. In English, we speak of being 'fresh as a daisy'—whereas in French, one is 'fresh as a rose'. Our ideas of freshness not only correspond to just-blooming flowers and complexions but to the feeling of crisp cleanliness that thorough house-cleaning implies.

After a hard winter, as the air warms up and spring's arrival is felt, a desire for freshness invades our souls. We feel the urge to get out our mops and spring clean the house from top to bottom. Surprisingly enough, upon opening the broom closet, the very things we use to clean our house give inspiration for its floral embellishment. Plants in nature are often referred to as 'scrub' or 'brush' and it is interesting to apply these adjectives to flowers. Sponges suggest celosias, brushes inspire papyrus plants, scrubbers evoke dahlias and kniphofias resemble brooms—and vice-versa. As unusual as they are appealing, such spic and span flowers radiate unconventional messages of freshness.

Perhaps the key to flowers' freshness is this unselfconscious beauty that makes them brighten any corner, any decor, any outfit. Vita Sackville-West, the consummate gardener and garden writer, wrote in her poem, The Garden: Spring:'

How fair the flowers unaware
That do not know what beauty is!
Fair, without knowing they are fair,
With poets and gazelles they share
Another world than this.[4] ■

Notes

[1] **Colette**
Pour un Herbier
Mermod, Lausanne, 1948
Editions Fayard, 1991

[2] **ibid**

[3] **ibid**

[4] **Brown**, Jane
Vita's Other World
A Gardening Biography of
V. Sackville-West
Penguin Books,
Harmondsworth, 1985

Other sources

Robinson, W.
The English Flower Garden
John Murray, London, 1899

De la Tour, Charlotte
Le Language des Fleurs
Garnier Frères, Paris, 1845

Prevost, Claude L.
A la Campagne
Gallimard Jeunesse
Paris, 1994

In the Occident, it is camomile that brings out blond highlights or walnut that colours hair a rich brown. Like golden grain or sheaves of straw, when a harvest of vegetal-dyed hair is randomly arranged, tousled as if by the wind and the elements, it resembles the plant from which it came, as if fresh from the fields, dry and fibrous, with the smell of sunlight and earth still clinging to warm tresses. A feeling for dry matter emerges and captures our senses, using seed-pods, lichens, dried grasses and flowers to create a soft yet highly textured fabric from which to knit or weave warm sweaters or scarves, nest-like couches or cushions.

Dry does not mean dead—far from it. Elements that have been properly dried can remain for millennia, as attested by the wheat grains and even blossom necklaces found intact in Egyptian tombs. But even the inevitable death of a flower or a plant can bring with it a strange and poignant beauty that tells us as much about matter and life as the just-bursting bud. Each cycle of life is intended to be studied and praised, for to ignore the loveliness in withering and dying, even if just for a season, is to miss out on a fundamental function of nature. Isn't the frost-covered blossom all the more beautiful because we know that it will remain so only for an instant before dying? Nobuyoshi Araki, the notable Japanese photographer, began photographing flowers during his wife's struggle with terminal cancer. To this day, he has created thousands of photos of flowers in varying stages of decline, explaining, 'I am more interested in flowers which are nearing their death than those at the beginning of their life. It sounds strange when I say they look lively, but they become very sensual.

I cannot say for sure that dying is more beautiful than living, but I feel that the beauty of flowers in a dying state is doubled. . . . I am very interested in mixing life and death in my compositions. By doing so, death becomes brighter and life becomes more erotic.'

Each element of organic matter—from the fresh blossom to the golden leaf, from the bright new sprout to the dark undergrowth dissolving into the soil—is worthy material, necessary to the generation and regeneration of the planet. Each is a treasure trove of possibility, inspiring man and providing him with raw material to continue creating, hopefully improving more than destroying the wealth of matter that nature has given us. ∎

Notes

[1] **Herbstreuth**, Peter
"Eros and Body"
Trans. John S. Southard
In *Transplant, Living Vegetation in Contemporary Art*
Ed. Barbara Nemitz
Hatje Cantz
Ostfildern-Ruit, Germany, 2000

[2] **Chipp**, Herschel B.
Theories of Modern Art
University of California Press
Berkeley and Los Angeles
USA, 1968

[3] **Garcia**, Michel
De la Garance au Pastel
Edisud Nature
Aix-en-Provence, France, 1996

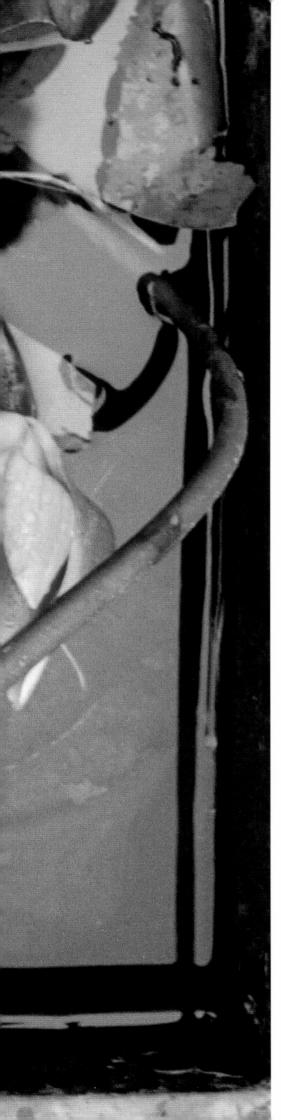

the new
art nouveau

and natural versus virtual

The more immaterial we will become, the more naturally we will want to live. Computer technology and information access will enable us to live a near-archaic style of life; with a flexible work ethic will come the circle of family and friends, together living much closer to the earth.

A hundred years ago it was the fear of industrialisation that drove us into the arms of Mother Nature; today, we again seek refuge to counterbalance the virtualisation of the planet. Exactly like a century ago, at the turn of the millennium man turns to nature for inspiration. Vases are derived from bulbs, roots and cacti, colours are designed by nature and prints are a replica of the real thing: flowers. Design becomes decorative and patterns get organised in movement; lines are fluid and volume studies the organic.

Even industrial design lends its shape from flower and leaf constructions, its plastics are coloured to resemble green hosta leaves, blue hydrangeas or orange petunias and its materials mimic succulent softness. A concept car might look like an exotic fruit on wheels, a blender starts to resemble a spiralling palm leaf, a chair is the mirror image of an anthurium.

Next to and together with industrial design, we see a rebirth of Arts and Crafts, to be able to obtain the one-of-a-kind, to experience the unique. Shapes are random and round and irregular, finishes are uneven and lively, stained, weathered or decayed. Patterns are hand-drawn and painted, in cut velvets or jacquard knits, patch-worked and over-embroidered, quilted and beaded. The rhythm in design is fluid and botanical, the lines are elongated and expressive, like plants reaching for the sky – aspiring to higher goals.

This is why garden tools and gardening clothes like aprons become an object of desire and decoration; this is why botanical matter translates into haberdashery, this is why eerily floating lotus flowers embrace a pond like embroidery embraces transparency. Design by nature is becoming a blooming business!

- L.E.

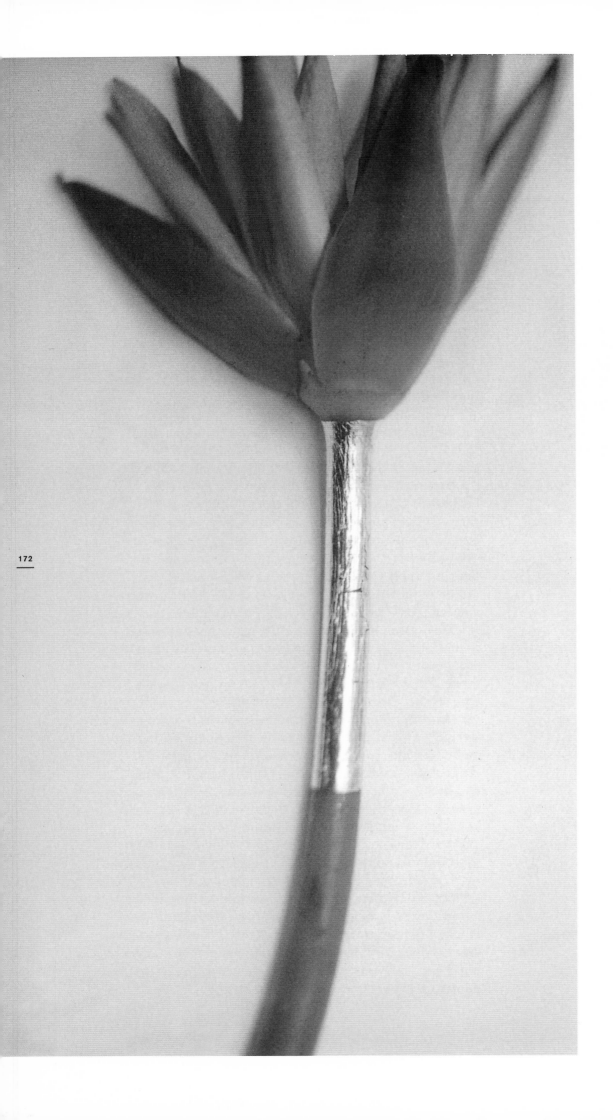

art de Nouveau . . . once
again. A tingling title to
arouse our curiosity and an
awareness that parallels can
be drawn between a trend lasting
from the end of the 19th century to
just prior to World War I and our
fledgling millennium, with its own
load of turbulent social events. If
Art Nouveau was initially launched
as a protest against the industrial
revolution, our third millennium
version is the retort to an excess of
immaterial and virtual people,
places, profits and property. Each
period has its own expressions—in
the case of Art Nouveau, they were
as numerous as varied—but what
interests us particularly is an over-
all, comparative scrutiny of *then*
and *now.*

Then, Art Nouveau was a widespread movement. It is important to
emphatically stress, however, that it
was not a style.[1] No particular school
symbolized it and its expressions
ranged from sinuous, floral patterns,
paintings and sculpture to geometric,
checkerboard designs. The common
denominator to them all was revolt:
against the hodgepodge of inexorable,
claustrophobic clutter, consummate
lack of taste and established order
in the realm of fine and applied arts
which characterized the Victorian
epoch. A period which combined
influences from all others, be it
Gothic, Renaissance or antiquity. A
testimony to this artistic disorder
was the lament of Alfred de Musset
who remarked, in 1836, that they
were living in all centuries except
their own, surrounded by debris of
the past as if the end of the world
was at hand.[2]

The veritable spawning of the Art
Nouveau movement can be attributed
to William Morris, English engraver,
craftsman, poet and socializing
politician (1834-1896), whose
uncompromising stance against the
industrial revolution served as a
basis and inspiration for those who
ultimately created the new movement.

Morris' standpoint was adamant
in its condemnation of the machine
and all it represented: humanity was
losing its soul and that was due to the
automation of the said revolution.
Indeed, mass production of items
devalued a certain quality of life, all
the more so since the manufactured
goods were so cheap. Whereas in the
past the contact between artisan and
the object he forged created an
esthetic and emotional bond, the
relationship between worker and
machine had little appeal and no
seeming virtue, other than that of
producing at less cost and providing
a job, albeit tedious, for the laborer.
These latter considerations were of
little, if any, relevance to Morris,
who focused more on big lines and
the general destruction of family
and social fiber resulting from this
recent and mechanized way of existence. Morris also attempted to
reduce the harmful social fracture
between patrons and workers, which
he perceived as the cause of many
ills. His own principles were rooted
in the Middle Ages whose values he
theoretically extolled — and although
romanticized, his notion of the free
and happy medieval craftsman did
manage to catch on among a pletho-
ra of followers, including painters
and architects as well as artisans.
Morris, Marshall, Faulkner and Co.
was founded in 1861 and included
associates Burne-Jones, Rossetti and
Webb. It became known as the Arts &
Crafts movement, promoting organic form and Gothic lines.

Another determining factor in
forging this new wave's image was
Japanese-inspired art. From mid
19th century on, a myriad of prints,
engravings, fans, kimonos, ceramics
and other objects inundated
Europe, reaching a culminating
point during the Universal
Exhibition in Paris, in 1867.

Of tremendous importance was the fact that Japanese artists gleaned their inspiration directly from nature: they illustrated the subtle poetry of nature's tones, cherry blossoms, water-lilies, bamboo and other undulating elements. Regardless of what they depicted, however, the crucial point was their scrutiny of nature and its use as a basis for their art, a contagious commitment which rapidly spread to their Occidental peers. Although a distinction should be made between art deriving from nature alone and art with an Oriental touch, all branches of Art Nouveau expression —typography, painting, prints, design, fabrics, tapestry, glass engraving, sculpture and architecture—displayed as such nature's mark.

Starting in England, where it was also known as 'Modern Style', it then spread like wildfire to other coun- ries, under other pseudonyms and whose variations, even within a given country, were revealing of the way it was perceived as well as practiced: 'Jugendstil' but also 'Lilienstil' meaning 'lily style', 'Wellenstil' for 'wave style' and a more denigrating term, 'Bandwurmstil' or 'tapeworm style' in Germany and 'Secession' in Austria; 'Stile Liberty' (after the famous store in London); 'Stile Floreale' (floral) or 'Stile Nouille' and 'Stile Vermicelli', both for noo- lles, in Italy; 'Modernismo' in Spain; 'Nieuwe Kunst' in the Netherlands and 'Paling stijl' for eels, in Belgium. In France, local appellations flourished as well: the 'Style Métro', inspired by the Metro entrances of Hector Guimard, or the 'Glasgow Style', after the Charles Mackintosh group.

Regardless of one's personal opinion of Art Nouveau, it should conceivably be considered, on one hand, as a kind of phenomenon whose indisputable and ultimate merit was to bring to a closing an otherwise desperately unsightly period; and on the other, as a search—successful or not—for an humane answer to a change of such magnitude that it appeared to threaten the very fiber of existence as man had known until that moment in time. . . .

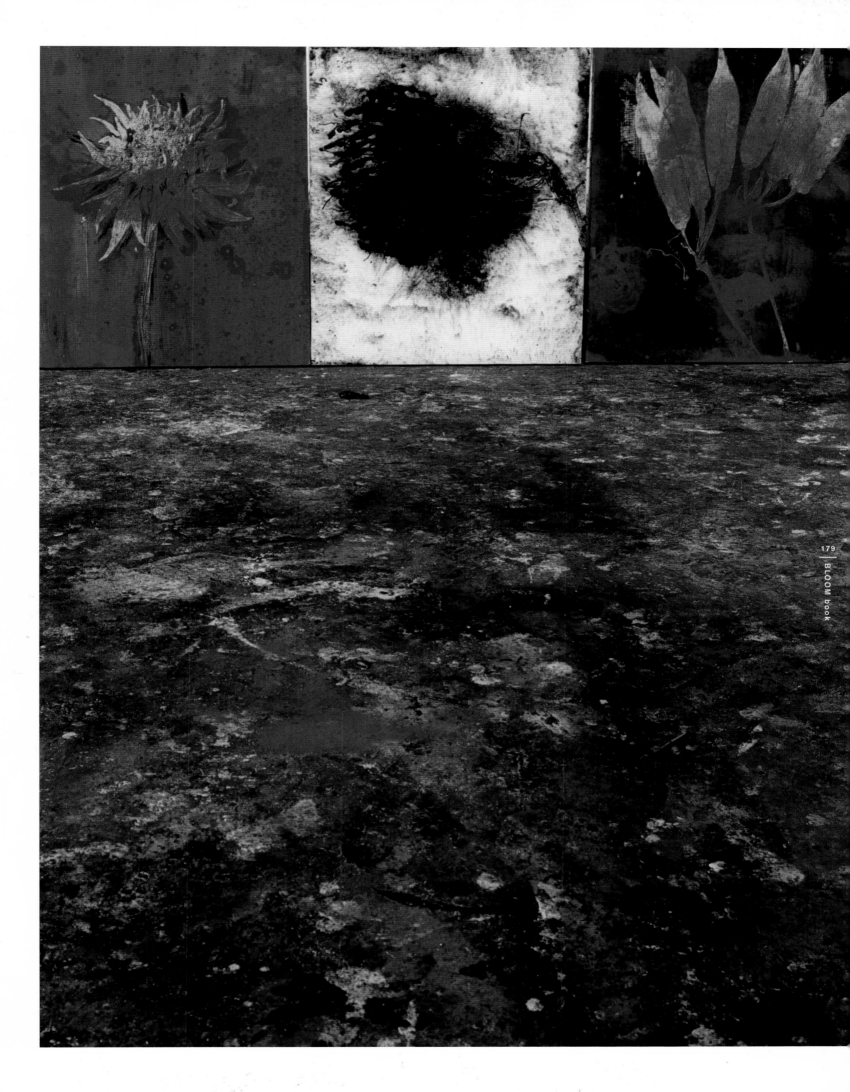

and all because of the machines that man himself invented.

Which brings us to *now*. Times are very different than a hundred years ago, and yet . . .

We've had ample time to digest the machine, learning to have it serve us rather than the other way around. Our so-called 'quality of life' has, for many populations, vastly improved, though not everyone has benefited from our know-how. Man has managed to create another useful but infernal machine, the computer. We've mastered communications and managed to make life so technically innovative, with such high performance, that one wonders if man still has a role to play on his own stage.

The struggle against what can be perceived as a kind of lack of humanity in our daily lives, against loss of contact among human beings—barricaded, as it were, behind our computer screens—is reminiscent, albeit without his medieval mythology, of Morris and his ideals. Even in design, renowned icon Philippe Starck, always conscious of the need to provide quality and style in products for the masses at more accessible prices, recently stated in an interview that 'more is more'. He realized that always giving priority to inexpensive goods was having a detrimental effect upon the fine work of craftsmen whose existence was menaced by too much of a good, cheap thing. Now he is designing as well more expensive items to be handmade by chosen artisans, to ensure that their traditions, knowledge and trades continue.

A condition specific to our times, inconceivable a century ago, is the virtualization resulting from our computerized existences, where the boundaries between real and make-believe are often blurred. Not surprisingly then, like our predecessors a hundred years ago, we turn to a tangible value for our inspiration: the flower.

Design is being created in collaboration with artisans and artists. Of course, this time around things are different, not as factual but more inspirational, not as rigid but more in motion, not as law-abiding but a bit more rebellious. The creative consumer, increasingly sure of his taste and talents, continues to invent ways to mix flowers with food, jewels with plants and blossoms with beads. The synergy of horticulture and culture is becoming more evident as we go.

The plant and flower boom is more than just a passing craze. The sensuality of plants is reassuring; their very presence is a small victory against ambient noise and visual pollution. . . . Perfect antidotes for daily stress and cybernetic non-existence. Since we don't want to leave our gardens behind when we finish toiling, we take them with us thanks to our garments. The apron becomes multi-purpose: it's an outer layer of clothing to prevent the others from becoming dirty, with deep pockets that can also be used for storing everything from trowels to handkerchiefs, money and portable telephones. It's a friendly garment which can be deployed and worn as one likes, in whatever fabric one chooses, rustic or transparent, to protect or parade, depending upon the occasion. Fabric can also take on the volume of flowers, for when we cannot grace our lapels with live blossoms, textile corsages can express our *art de nouveau* tendencies.

Each epoch masters its mutations and distress as best it can. Beauty and art have always been safeguards against whatever is ailing, or assailing, us. However, the ultimate, reassuring source of comfort and inspiration, the one common, esthetic denominator to all times, in all circumstances, is nature. As Shakespeare said, '. . . The art itself is nature'.∎

Cora

Notes

[1] **Duncan**, Alastair
Art Nouveau
Thames & Hudson, Paris, 2000

[2] **ibid**

Other sources

Hofstatter, Hans H.
Jugenstil et Art Nouveau,
Œuvres Graphiques
Albin Michel, Paris 1985

Symboles en Fleurs, les Fleurs
dans l'Art autour de 1900
Catalogue de l'Exposition à
l'Institut Néerlandais
(30 sept -28 nov 1999)
Snoeck-Ducaju & Fils, Gand

captions

and credits

Cover **The sculptural dahlia**
photo Yoshiaki Tsutsui

Page(s)

4 **A return to nature**
*aprons created for BLOOM
magazine by* Margareth Häusler
photo Michael Baumgarten
styling Jessica Hayns

6 **Ypomoea: a fertility symbol**
photo Lon van Keulen

7 **Getting in touch with our roots**
*aprons created for BLOOM
magazine by* Margareth Häusler
photo Michael Baumgarten
styling Jessica Hayns

8-9 **An eye for potatoes**
photos Lon van Keulen

10-11 **Sinuous beauty**
vases by Jonathan Adler
photos Cora
styling Nelson Sepulveda

12-13 **The gracefully unusual
Cyclamen graecum**
photo & styling Nelson Sepulveda
& Evelyne Boogaert

14-17 **Vases inspired by gourds**
photos Philippe Munda
styling Nelson Sepulveda &
Ludovine Billaud

18-19 **Elevating the humble potato**
plate prototypes for Lunéville
in BLOOM
photos Daniel Schweizer

20-21 **Knitting nature**
*vase covers created for
BLOOM magazine by*
Shirin Heezen
photos Michael Baumgarten

22-23 **An endless variety of bulbs**
photos Sarah Allen

24-25 **Iris & Odontocidium roots**
photos Cora
styling Nelson Sepulveda

26-27 **A vivid green chrysanthemum**
photo Philippe Costes

28-29 **The generous leaves of the
Gunnera manicata**
photos MAP/Yann Monel

30-33 **Green grass galore**
*pants & aprons created for
BLOOM magazine by*
Renate van Beynum
photos Sandrine Expilly

34-35 **An organic green Christmas**
photo Philippe Munda
styling Christian Kleeman

36-37 **The Emerald Rose®**
vase by François Duris
photos Michael Baumgarten

38-39 **The green amaryllis**
photo Lon van Keulen

40-41 **Leafy inspiration 1**
photo Valeska Gräfenstein

42-43 **Leafy inspiration 2**
painting by Margareth Häusler
photos Michael Baumgarten

44 **A tender hosta**
photo Thomas Straub

45 **Hosta couture**
clothes by Adeline André haute
couture
photo Philippe Munda

46-49 **The healing beauty of flowers**
pressed flowers by Elisabeth Heim
photos Thomas Straub
styling Laurence Brabant &
Veerle Hommelen

50 **Tinted Alcea & blackberry lips**
photo Marcel Van Der Vlugt
styling Evelyne Boogaert
make-up Philippe Miletto @ House
of Orange

51 **Lucious Rosa & strawberry lips**
photo Marcel Van Der Vlugt
styling Evelyne Boogaert
make-up Philippe Miletto @ House
of Orange

52 **The elixer of dew**
latex cups by Laurent Brabant
photo Bruno Poinsard

53 **The beauty of dew**
photo Thomas Straub
model Lucie Rottova @ NEXT
make-up Ingrid Stockreiter @ OLGA
hair CARITA by Tom

54 **The energy of dew**
photo Bruno Poinsard

55 **Youth dew**
photo Thomas Straub
model Lucie Rottova @ NEXT
make-up Ingrid Stockreiter @ OLGA

56-57 **Parfums à boire – perfumes
for the palate**
photos Daniel Schweizer
styling Nelson Sepulveda

58 **Epidermic inspiration 1**
latex vases by Laurence Brabant
photo Noëlle Hoeppe
styling Nelson Sepulveda

59-60 **Epidermic inspiration 2:
Paeonia & iris**
photo Noëlle Hoeppe
styling Nelson Sepulveda

61 **Epidermic inspiration 3**
latex vases by Laurence Brabant
photo Noëlle Hoeppe
styling Nelson Sepulveda

62 **A second skin**
dress knitting & design
Christiane Gestrich
photo Thomas Straub
styling Nelson Sepulveda
model Rottova @ NEXT
make-up Ingrid Stockreiter @ OLGA
hair CARITA by Tom

63 **Flower or flesh?**
photo Sonia Ana Lievain

64-67 **The honey treatment**
photos Thomas Straub
styling Nelson Sepulveda
make-up Ingrid Stockreiter @ OLGA
model Eliane @ NEXT

68 **A north-south-east-west
composition**
photo Cora
styling Nelson Sepulveda

70 **Ranunculus, skimmia,
amaranthus & iris**
photo Sacha van Dorssen
styling Nelson Sepulveda

71 **Still life**
photo Sacha van Dorssen
styling Nelson Sepulveda

72-73 **Associating iris & aloe**
photo Sacha van Dorssen
styling Nelson Sepulveda

74 **Grey and whitened tones**
felt & latex pots by Yves Andrieux
photo Thomas Straub

75 **Old and new elements**
wood & latex pots by Yves Andrieux
photo Thomas Straub

76 **Composition in white**
photo Michael Baumgarten
styling Christian Kleeman

77 **An assembly of textures**
ceramics by Anne Musso
photo Michael Baumgarten
styling Christian Kleeman

78-79 **A ceramic garden**
ceramics by Nathalie Lété
photos Michael Baumgarten
styling Nelson Sepulveda

80 **Couture culture**
photo Mariëlle Leenders

81 **Carnation inspiration**
choker by Anne Prudhomme
photo Valerie Knight
model Caroline @ FAM

82-85 **The compositions of the Brokpa**
photos Michael Wooley

86 **'Face du sauveur n°10'**
painting by Alexej von Jawlensky
© ADAGP, Paris 2001

87 **A palette of roses**
photo Michael Baumgarten

88-89 **Australian banksia and protea flowers**
photos Sonia Ana Lievain

90-91 **Composing floral soups**
photos Noëlle Hoeppe
styling Nelson Sepulveda
assisted by Manon Gignoux,
Celine Devisme & Lydia Raev

92-95 **Helianthus**
photos Sonia Ana Lievain

96 **Dahlia dance**
photo Yoshiaki Tsutsui

97 **Watanabe's sartorial flowers**
photo Thomas Straub
styling Carin Scheve

98-99 **The sculptural dahlia**
photo Yoshiaki Tsutsui

100-101 **Tulipa 'Blue Herom' & bulb vases**
photos Cora
styling Nelson Sepulveda &
Evelyne Boogaert

102 **Heliconia**
photo Henri Bourne
styling Graham Hollick

103 **Georgia O'Keeffe stamp**
design © 1995 U.S. Postal Service
photograph of red poppy © 1927
Malcom Varon, NYC (reproduced
with permission)

104-105 **Nelumbo & Papaver: nature & sculpture**
photos Henri Bourne
styling Graham Hollick

106-107 **Gourd & cocoa pod**
photos Peter Knaup

108-109 **Inner & outer volumes**
photos Michael Baumgarten

110-113 **Flower memorials from the Montparnasse cemetery**
photos Lon van Keulen

114-115 **Photograms**
Hélène Purcell

116-117 **Desert plants from the Huntington Gardens**
photos Ron van Dongen

118 **Fresh market flowers**
photo Sonia Ana Lievain

119-121 **Garden bouquets**
photos Claudia Van Ryssen

122-123 **Nasturtium & hydrangea wrapping**
photos Sonia Ana Lievain

124 **A friendly market face**
photo Sonia Ana Lievain

125 **Lily of the valley**
photo Frédéric de Gasquet

126-127 **Tools inspired by orchids**
by Annekatrien van Meegen
photos Cora

128-129 **Helleborus**
photo Sylvie Becquet
styling Christian Kleeman

130-131 **Spring has sprung**
photos Cora
styling Nelson Sepulveda &
Veerle Hommelen

132-133 **Spring cleaning with celosia & kniphofia**
photos Martin Mulder @ NEL
styling John Biesheuvel

134-135 **Sprucing up the everyday**
photo Sarah Allen

136-137 **An armful of wildflowers**
photo Paul Bellaart @ Tavern Agency
styling Gert van der Keuken &
Catharina van Eetvelde
model Erike Lucas @ FAM

138-140 **Atlantic blues: agapanthus, delphinium & hydrangea**
photos Koto Bolofo
styling Evelyne Boogaert & Carin
Scheve

141 **Cyclamen persicum takes a drink**
photo Lon Van Keulen

142 **Delphinium decor**
clothes & spangles created by
Christiane Gestrich
photo Sabine Pigalle

143 **Delphinium**
photo Michael Baumgarten

144-145 **Deep purple**
photo Michael Baumgarten
styling Nelson Sepulveda

146-147 **The sensual peony**
photos Noëlle Hoeppe
styling Christian Kleeman

148-149 **The beauty of dying flowers**
photos Nobuyoshi Araki

150-151 **Porcelain rose**
photo Carmen Rodriguez

152-153 **Inventing new carnation hybrids**
photos Michael Baumgarten
styling Nelson Sepulveda

154-155 **Waves of grain**
photos Philippe Salomon
hair CARITA by Jean-Claude Gallon
@ Elite

156-157 **Carnation & protea prototypes**
photos Don Freeman
styling Graham Hollick

158-159 **Cameo textures & colours**
dress & tablecloth created by
Margareth Haüsler
photos Philippe Munda
styling Nelson Sepulveda

160-161 **Chocolate-covered orchid on cocoa cake**
photo Bruno Poinsard

162-163 **Bejewelled by frost**
photos Marion Nickig @ Green
Picture Brokers

164-165 **The metallic Nepenthes & Peperomia caperata**
photos Lon van Keulen
styling Nelson Sepulveda

166-167 **The cuddly Verbascum bombyciferum**
photo Lon van Keulen

168-169 **A dry tie**
scarf created by Côme Touvay
photos Michael Baumgarten
styling Nelson Sepulveda
model K-mel @ PH-one

170-171 **Water lilies**
photo Sarah Allen

172-175 **Botanical jewels**
photos Philippe Munda
concept Studio Edelkoort for
Vogue Gioiello reprinted with
permission of Vogue Gioiello

176-177 **Inner corsage**
jacket by Marion Hanania
photos Michael Baumgarten
model Savanna @ FAM

178 **Doryanthes excelsa**
photo Peter Knaup

179 **Inspired by flowers**
paintings by Thomas Fougeirol
photo Michel Dubois

180-181 **A rose is a rose . . .**
rose preserves by Le Creuset des
saveurs / Jacques Rimbault
photos Michael Baumgarten
styling Nelson Sepulveda

182-183 **Notions of nature**
photos Julie Chloé Degueldre
styling Delphine Chailloux

184-185 **Tacca chantrierei**
photos Cora
styling Evelyne Boogaert

186 **Soothing nature**
photo Michael Baumgarten

187 **Garden couture**
apron created for BLOOM
magazine by Margareth Haüsler
photo Michael Baumgarten
styling Jessica Hayns
model Margareth

188 **Apron fashion**
apron created for BLOOM
magazine by Margareth Haüsler
photo Michael Baumgarten
styling Jessica Hayns
model Mika Florian @ NEXT

189 **Begonia rex motifs**
photo Michael Baumgarten

103 Please note:
Georgia O'Keeffe,
Red Poppy, 1927
© Adagp, Paris 2001

Art Direction
Lidewij Edelkoort
Anthon Beeke

Graphic Design
Anthon Beeke
Jeroen Jas

Text
Li Edelkoort
Lisa White
With the participation
of Judith Helm

Creative Direction
Nelson Sepulveda

Editorial Direction
Ghislaine Bavoillot

Editorial Managers
Nathalie Démoulin
Lisa White

Copyeditor
Kathryn Lancaster

Floral Direction
Evelyne Boogaert

Production
Christian Poirier
Jeanne-Marie Charles
Zahia Hebbir

Fabrication
Tatiana Nadin
Murielle Vaux

Thank you to
Henri Moulié
Ryu Kubota
Capucine
le Jardin de Bellevue
l'Atelier Vert
Olivier Bennato

© Flammarion
Paris, 2001

ISBN
2-08010-623-6

Numéro d'édition
FA0623-01-VIII

Dépôt légal
October 2001

Lithography
Colorset bv
The Netherlands

Printing
Canale, Italy

Flammarion
26 rue Racine
75006 Paris

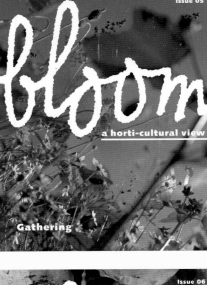

to order a **single copy**
DM 90 - FF 300 - US$ 55
Lit. 90.000 - £ 36 - Dfl. 100
+ postage

to order a **subscription**
to **BLOOM**, 2 books per annum
DM 165 - FF 560 - US$ 105
Lit. 165.000 - £ 60 - Dfl. 190
incl. postage

DM 225 - FF 745 - US$ 140
Lit. 225.000 - £ 85 - Dfl. 250
incl. airmail

please place your orders at
United Publishers S.A.
30, Boulevard Saint Jacques
75014 Paris, France
T +33 (0)1 44 08 68 98
F +33 (0)1 43 31 77 91
info@unitedpublishers.com

if you enjoyed the Bloom Book, we invite you to subscribe to Bloom magazine

144 pages of new photos and text, published every spring and fall

Back issues available!